ELTON JOHN

A BIOGRAPHY

ELTON JOHN

Barry Toberman

WEIDENFELD AND NICOLSON

LONDON

PICTURE ACKNOWLEDGEMENTS

The photographs in this book are reproduced by permission of the following:

Syndication International Ltd 1, 2 (top), 3, 4, 5 (below), 6, 8; *Rex Features* 2 (below), 5 (top), 7

Published in Great Britain by
George Weidenfeld & Nicolson Limited
91 Clapham High Street
London SW4 7TA

This paperback edition published by
George Weidenfeld & Nicolson Limited 1989

ISBN 0 297 79646 1

Printed by Guernsey Press Co Ltd, Guernsey, C.I.

For Sue and Annalise

Acknowledgements

The author wishes to thank the following for their time and assistance – Kiki Dee, Roger Greenaway, Andy and George Hill, Bill Johnson, Keith Mercer, Mick Randall, Ray Williams and the many others from the worlds of entertainment and sport whose uncredited contributions were equally invaluable.

Thanks also to Lesley for the additional research, Sue for the word processing, Gerald, Jane and Sharon for advice and encouragement and Frank Lovece for American guidance.

The efficiency of staff at the British Newspaper, Lincoln Center (New York) and Camden libraries is gratefully acknowledged. Ditto for the Museum of Broadcasting, New York, and Virgin Video.

Special thanks to my parents.

Foreword

Reggie Dwight's schooboy dreams were nothing out of the ordinary – playing on Wimbledon's Centre Court, scoring a goal at Wembley (as his cousin actually did) and emulating the achievements of the American rock 'n' roll legends whose records he mimed to in his bedroom.

Although he failed to make the Centre Court, his competitive partners have included Billie Jean King and Jimmy Connors. While Wembley as a player was never a remote possibility, he became the chairman of a club which reached an FA Cup Final in 1984, and almost repeated the feat three years later. As for Jerry Lee Lewis and Little Richard, young Reggie Dwight did not grow up to equal their achievements. He way surpassed them.

A change of name to Elton John, a fortuitous introduction to a seventeen-year-old Lincolnshire poet called Bernie Taupin and a felicitous switch from penning songs for others to composing for himself sowed the seeds for the launch of the world's most successful recording artist of the early to mid 1970s.

A star who in a four-year time-span released seven consecutive American number one LPs. A charismatic stage performer whose adoring audiences have ranged from 400,000 in New York to a Moscow auditorium filled largely with selected party functionaries. A pianist of classical training whose dextrous playing is admired by experts.

He was the first superstar of the rock era not to look the part – the antithesis, in fact. However, deficiencies in hair and matinée-idol physiognomy were more than compensated by an amalgam of talent and stage costumery.

A backstage gift has always been the capacity to bounce back from adversity. From as far back as 1971, musical obituaries have returned to haunt their writers.

In 1976, the wisdom of Elton's admission of bi-sexuality was widely questioned, particularly as he had only just assumed the chairmanship of Watford Football Club. His career survived the revelation as did his position as a soccer executive. To the surprise of the majority, he has been anything but an absentee figurehead at Watford, industriously discharging his chairman's duties.

More recently the subject of damaging popular press accusations about his private life, he promised – and delivered – legal retribution.

In contradiction to the acres of newsprint filled globally with engaging or controversial quotes, there is an intensely private side to Elton's character. Remember, all but a handful of the innumerable words he has sung so eloquently represent the thoughts and fantasies of others. The only child of an unhappy marriage, he has, by his own admission, felt acutely alone at moments of undreamt of accomplishment. Two suicide attempts were described as pleas for attention.

At other times, he has preferred the company of inanimate objects to the presence of humans. Certainly, Elton largely blamed himself for the failure of his marriage to recording engineer, Renate Blauel. His record collection is said to be the equal of any private library; his works of art the envy of specialist buyers. Not only is Elton acquisitive. Once bought, never dispensed with – at least until the massive Sotheby's sale of possessions weird and wonderful. He has confessed that to him, even the potential disposal of a 1970 T-shirt represents a crisis of conscience.

The twentieth anniversary of the release of the Beatles' *Sergeant Pepper* coincided with Elton's completion of two decades in the music industry. From the same generation, only McCartney, the Stones and Bowie can exceed or match his longevity at the pinnacle of popular taste.

Yet Elton was confiding retirement plans to journalists as far back as 1971. Since then, the date of his rock 'n' roll pension has been the subject of constant revision. He could not foresee himself playing 'Crocodile Rock' when he was thirty – then thirty-four, thirty-seven and thirty-eight.

When he appeared at Live Aid in 1985, the quality of his performance bore rigorous comparison with any other on the transatlantic bill comprising the most glittering array of musical talent ever set before an audience. Despite his subsequent throat problems, Elton was again in his element in Australia at concerts with the Melbourne Symphony Orchestra. Now fully recovered, he has returned with gusto to the recording and concert fray.

Professionally, there is precious little left to achieve – although nothing would give him greater pleasure than to record a solo British number one single.

Once questioned on how he envisioned himself at sixty, Elton responded: 'Playing "Your Song" in a pub somewhere, basking in ancient glory and being yelled at for not playing current hits.' With a considerable personal fortune, estimated at £42 million by a financial journal prior to the Sotheby's auction, he could certainly afford to if that was the contemporary motivation.

Whatever his future path, the likelihood is that Elton will continue to confound his critics – and probably himself.

Reg Strikes Back could not have been a more apposite choice for the title of Elton John's 1988 album. Not only was the nomenclature accurate in a musical sense, as the LP brought him back to commercial favour on both sides of the Atlantic.

The title exemplified the admirable resilience of the erstwhile Reg Dwight in times of personal and professional difficulty.

Certainly, the preceding year would have tested the fortitude of the strongest of characters, let alone one constantly in the public eye – and a regular target for tabloid press sniping.

Indeed Elton described the winter of 1987 as 'the worst five months of my life.' Though not averse to the melodramatic declaration, the star had genuine cause for concern as his luxuriant 'Yellow Brick Road' appeared under imminent threat of demolition.

Elton's career, health, marriage and image all came under the microscope. Far from life beginning at 40, seemingly everything he touched turned to sensationalist banner newspaper headlines.

Amid incessant rumours of a career threatening malady, a straightforward operation in Australia cured a throat ailment which had plagued him through a typically exhaustive concert itinerary. In truth, Elton was under greater threat back in Britain.

A determinedly salacious 'exclusive' series in The Sun contained highly unsavoury allegations about his personal life. The accusations were strenuously denied and a series of writs issued against the newspaper.

Though the star's only short-term consolation was a heartening groundswell of public support, Elton eventually extracted seven-figure recompense in a record libel settlement in December 1988, the newspaper admitting that the stories were completely untrue.

Even Elton's stewardship of his beloved Watford Football Club – a haven of sanity during past career and private crises – merited close scrutiny.

Acknowledged as one of the clubs best geared to family support in the Football League, Watford's homely image was a source of pride to the star. But it was on the pitch that Watford had really prospered under Elton's chairmanship.

Probably his most crucial footballing accomplishment was to persuade Graham Taylor to become Watford manager in 1977. Under Taylor, the club rose from Division Four to within grasp of the First Division title, qualified for European competition and reached an FA Cup Final.

Moreoever, Watford seemed likely to provide the sole shaft of light in Elton's winter of discontent by again reaching the last four of England's premier cup competition. However, in the week of the losing semi-final against tournament favourites, Spurs, Elton found his troubles transferring from the front pages to the sports columns.

In this instance, the reportage proved of factual foundation.

Vehemently denied at the time, the story – that Elton was on the verge of selling the club – was validated later in the year with the announcement that Robert Maxwell's British Printing and Communication Corporation had bought out his interest for £2 million. (The deal was later scrapped after a Football League edict prompted by the Maxwell family's involvement in a number of league clubs.)

But what really excited the public interest was the state of his unexpected marriage to recording engineer, Renate Blauel.

Renate had been conspicuously absent from Elton's hospital bedside in Australia, ostensibly because of American recording commitments.

Speculation heightened when Renate was again an absentee at Elton's glittering fortieth birthday extravaganza at the Rickmansworth home of his manager and confidant, John Reid. On this occasion, a guest list comprising Royalty and musical and showbiz counter-parts was overshadowed by Renate's non-appearance. Flu was cited as the explanation.

Elton's close friend and spasmodic singing partner, Kiki Dee, was a late arrival at the festivities, missing out on a midnight firework display sufficiently spectacular to curtail the sleep of a large section of the populace for miles around. Kiki found the man of the hour in surprisingly buoyant mood.

. 'He seemed a little subdued, but highly social nevertheless. Mind you, with four hundred people there in his honour, what else could he be?'

Lionel Richie, Phil Collins, George Michael, George Harrison, Ringo Starr, Elaine Paige, Sir John Mills and Peter Gabriel were among the stellar guest list. And the token gift for the man with almost everything? An £80,000 Ferrari Testarossa.

What Elton palpably lacked was a happy marriage. Official credence to months of gossip came in a brief statement the following morning.

Acknowledging that he and Renate had parted company, Elton stressed that the couple remained 'very good personal friends.'

He later said that Renate had reacted to the separation calmly and moved for a time to London in preference to Elton's palatial Windsor and Los Angeles homes. Before long, however, Elton was 'confiding' to a television audience of millions that they were back under the same roof.

With calculated candour, Elton used his appearance on Michael Parkinson's series of 'One to One' feature-length interviews to partially redress the negative balance of his tabloid media coverage.

Totally at ease in the talk show environment, he gave a masterful display, abetted by the sympathetic questioning of his good friend, and wedding guest, Parky.

When Elton alluded to attempts by the press to obtain medical information about him and Renate – 'they probably want to examine my sperm, God forbid' – the supportive response from the studio audience did more than illustrate the star's enormous popularity.

Public distaste for the relentless persecution of Elton John was evident even among readers of the paper largely responsible. The rumours from its Wapping base were that sales of The Sun dipped considerably on the days it led with allegations about Elton.

But there was undoubtedly widespread interest in the state of his rocky matrimonial affairs. Elton told Parkinson that Renate had temporarily returned to Windsor.

'We've been spending the week together,' he disclosed, adding: 'We're really good friends.' Above all, the latter statement summarized the true state of their relationship.

Within weeks, the marriage again made headlines – this time the press being told of a successful reconciliation.

In another textbook chat show performance, Elton apprised Terry Wogan that the most beneficial aspect of his cumulative troubles was that the personal 'crisis' had reunited him and Renate. 'I was just going through a bad patch in my life. It had nothing to do with her.' Probably so. Yet friends still considered Elton and Renate more akin to brother and sister than husband and wife. The feeling was that the marriage had in part been a concerted attempt by the star to embark upon a new lifestyle – with his desire to be a father a primary motive.

The couple shared a passionate involvement in the music business, a penchant for extravagant dressing and an undoubted admiration for one another.

A rock 'n' roll existence is hardly the basis of a conventional marriage. Nonetheless, the 'odd couple' – as friends christened them – fuelled speculation about the longevity of their union with extensive periods apart.

In a revealing interview, Elton admitted his culpability for the marriage's rocky path. His peripatetic working and social milieux was not the best foundation for domesticated bliss.

'We had a kitchen which took a year (to complete) but I was never there to see what was going on. I think she's a bit frightened of doing things without me being there because she doesn't know what my tastes are.' After years of marriage, 'we don't know whether we like the walls white or the walls blue.'

In true Elton style, there were periodic public displays of affection for his wife. A month past their fourth wedding anniversary, he threw Renate a no-expense-spared birthday party at the exclusive London nightspot, Brown's.

But with even Royal invitations being accepted on a solo basis (Elton arrived alone at Buckingham Palace for Prince Charles' fortieth birthday celebration), the inevitable was only as far away as November 1988.

With Elton in Denmark, working on the successor to *Reg Strikes Back*, the announcement of an amicable break-up came from Renate.

The official version, issued on behalf of both parties, attributed the impending divorce to increasing periods of separation due to professional obligations.

'Both of us have been, and will be, so busy with our work commitments that we are seeing too little of each other. For this reason, it seems unavoidable that we are growing apart.

'We are, however, parting on the most amicable terms and genuinely intend to remain the best of friends.'

Renate added: 'I wish Elton all the happiness in the world and I know he wishes me the same.'

While the tabloid press speculated on the magnitude of the divorce settlement – Elton did not apparently follow the prevalent show business convention by signing a pre-nuptial agreement – no-one doubted that Renate would be lavishly provided for.

Indeed, the star's parting gift bore all the hallmarks of true affection. A 17th century cottage in Godalming, in the heart of the Surrey stockbroker belt, its name – 'Cobblers' – was straight out of the Elton catalogue, even if the choice was that of former owner, comedian, Billy Dainty. Renate's architect brother, Bernhard, was put in charge of improvements to the listed building.

There was, alas, a poignant postscript. The following February, the cottage was badly damaged by a fire, three days before the fifth anniversary of Elton and Renate's wedding.

Meanwhile, Elton was putting his personal unhappiness behind him in the most positive of ways. Symbolic of his fresh start was the almost simultaneous lifting of the slur on his character left by The Sun's lurid accusations.

A front-page splash in his tabloid adversary said almost all . . . 'Sorry Elton'. Ensuing came an apology unprecedented in its grovelling content and prominence.

The paper's volte-face on the eve of what would have been an enormously expensive series of legal actions even extended to its centre pages.

There, taking to extremes the sudden rapprochement, The Sun cooed in wonderment at Elton's 'amazing' diet which had seen him shed two stones in less than two months.

The background to the paper's gushing retraction was that the libel action for the last of its stories to hasten the star's lawyers into action – a totally groundless accusation that Elton had silenced 'vicious Rottweiler dogs' through surgery – was the first to be scheduled for a High Court hearing.

Faced with an embarrassing defeat which would arouse further sympathy for the star from a canine conscious public, The Sun cut its losses with its unreserved retractions on the morning of the case.

Nevertheless, this voluntary appeasement cost the paper £1 million in settlement of the libel damages.

The apology, agreed by Elton, quoted the star and Sun as 'delighted to announce that they have reached agreement for the resolution of all outstanding litigation between them.

'A series of front page and other articles in February 1987 made very grave allegations about Elton's private life and called him a liar.

'The Sun now accepts that there is no truth in any of these highly defamatory allegations. The paper also recognises the great distress these articles caused to Elton and apologises to him.'

The statement also encompassed an apology for the bark-less dogs allegation, which carried 'no truth whatsoever'.

With Elton quoted as saying life was too short to bear grudges, the only aggrieved party was the judge whose thunder had been stolen by the hurried friendship pact before a cosy audience of 13 million readers.

Though approving the deal – the biggest in British libel history – Mr Justice Michael Davies said the court had been 'manipulated' by the announcement of the result of the action before it had come to court.

Commenting that the courts were not 'a supine adjunct to a publicity machine for pop stars and newspapers,' the judge was moved to remark: 'Reading it, one would think that Elton John and the newspaper had formed a mutual admiration society.'

The judge was certainly correct in his assessment that 'the parties were determined to milk the situation in order to obtain the maximum publicity for both sides.'

Not that Elton John has ever seriously ailed from publicity deficiency.

Buoyed by his high profile vindication, he quietly forgot his earlier threats to move permanently to America. A great place to own a sumptuous residence, it lacks homely soccer clubs with Cinderella-style histories.

Elton's decision to sell Watford had come when at his lowest emotional ebb. Indeed events in the boardroom and on the pitch at the club's Vicarage Road premises only added to his torment.

The ill-starred projected sale of his interest in Watford to the BPCC was announced in November 1987, six months after Graham Taylor ended his productive association with the club by accepting the managership of Aston Villa.

Taylor's replacement, Dave Bassett (formerly boss at Wimbledon) was Elton's somewhat capricious choice, made against the wishes of many at the club.

Elton had exhibited both footballing and business acumen in pursuit of Bassett, who in theory had the virtues of local upbringing and residency.

A particularly shrewd move was an unforewarned visit to the Bassett household on FA Cup Final day in the full knowledge that his manager elect was at Wembley as part of the BBC commentary team.

It afforded the star a heaven-sent opportunity of selling his concept of Dave Bassett's place in the Vicarage Road grand scenario to the manager's wife, Christine.

Two days later, news of Bassett's appointment was announced at a press conference originally convened to promote another globe-trotting adventure – Watford FC's second tour of China.

Bassett paid testimony to the chairman's persuasive powers: 'Elton sold me the club with his enthusiasm. I have always admired Watford but never thought I would get the chance to manage them.'

Elton described the appointment as 'the start of a new era' for the club. The prophecy was borne out, but not in the mode chairman and manager desired. Bassett's reign was disastrous.

The best that can be said is that Watford finally won the cup – albeit the Great Wall Cup – through five victories in China.

And from the chairman's standpoint, the Oriental excursion had the supplementary benefit of accelerating his post-operative recuperation away from the public glare.

As on Watford's previous Chinese visit, Elton thrived in a country where, at worst, he would attract comment merely for examples of sartorial inelegance. For him, China offered the peerless virtue of an environment unsuited to the presence of hordes of insatiable gossip writers.

The insurmountable problem was that back in England, the team's winning ways deserted it.

With admirable loyalty, Elton stuck by his manager as Watford's fortunes plummeted. Eight months later he admitted his folly as Bassett departed with the club firmly rooted to the foot of the first division.

'It was my mistake to appoint him,' Elton confessed, going on to accept guilt for the unrest at what, hitherto, had been an oasis of contentment in the fractious world of football.

Acknowledging that Bassett's style and approach had divided the Watford board, the star felt he could have done more to restore unity.

'For that Dave has my sympathy. I stopped going to matches because I didn't have the sense to confront the people who were against him.'

Learning from his self-professed misjudgements, Elton ensured that Bassett's replacement had the perfect Watford credentials.

Brought as a player to Vicarage Road by Graham Taylor, Steve Harrison had graduated to first team coach under Taylor's tutelage and went with him to Villa.

Harrison arrived too late to save Watford from relegation, but his gradual reinvigoration of the club served to recharge the footballing batteries of its chairman.

So much so that he described his triumphant return to the concert stage in America as a means towards financing Watford's £700,000 summer expenditure in the transfer market and the possibility of future signings.

The US dates were the culmination of Elton's musical and physical rehabilitation after his throat operation. Even before *The Sun*'s libel pay-out, his financial status had been enhanced by the extensively publicized sale of his art, furniture and rock and pop memorabilia at Sotheby's.

Four days' sustained auctioneering brought in a cool £5 million. 'Kind of like watching your own death,' was the star's verdict.

Typical of any aspect of Elton's life, the projected auction captured the public's imagination.

A month before the diverse lots went under the hammer, fans, art connoisseurs and the simply intrigued flocked in their thousands to the Victoria and Albert Museum in Kensington for a pre-sale guide masquerading as an exhibition.

Rarely can V&A exhibits have been displayed accompanied by suggested price tags. Opinion among visitors divided as to whether the exercise had been innovative or tackily commercial.

Unarguably though, the advance publicity proved invaluable when the collection came to auction. The proceeds way surpassed Sotheby's own estimate of £3 million and virtually every item was sold.

Elsewhere, the cash registers were ringing for Elton from a more conventional source.

Prior to the release of *Reg Strikes Back*, he had returned to the singles listings on both sides of the Atlantic with a version of 'Candle In The Wind' culled from the live double album recorded with the Melbourne Symphony Orchestra.

From the same set, the release of 'Your Song' as a 45 turned his career full circle.

In contrast, his first studio LP for two years gave evidence of fresh creative impetus.

Written with Bernie Taupin, produced by Chris Thomas and recorded with the help of Pete Townshend, two Beach Boys and some familiar names from the star's first flush of fame, *Reg Strikes Back* whetted the appetite for Elton's US dates.

While achieving mildly encouraging sales in his homeland, the addictive single, 'I Don't Wanna Go On With You Like That', stormed to the top of the American listings.

Concert fans were equally ecstatic about the performing renaissance of Reg, nowhere more than at New York's Madison Square Garden, scene of some of Elton's finest hours – in particular, a memorable guest appearance by John Lennon.

Having painstakingly rebuilt his career, regenerated his football club, vanquished his newspaper tormentor and sorted out his personal life, all that remained was to mastermind a facelift to his mansion at Windsor, Berkshire.

Certainly, the Sotheby's sale of possessions exquisite and eccentric had provided the perfect excuse to start again.

So undeniably wealthier, theoretically wiser and purportedly slimmer, Elton's personal and professional affairs appeared in prime readiness for yet another new phase.

While life may not begin at forty, a jolt of renewal at forty-two cannot go amiss. And in Elton's case 'comeback' is a pejorative term as, for one reason or another, he has rarely been out of the headlines.

Back in 1975 on the autobiographical *Captain Fantastic* album, he described himself in song as hardly a hero, just someone his mother might know.

Mummy just look at him now.

E lton Hercules John was born Reginald Kenneth Dwight on 25 March 1947 in the safely Conservative London suburb of Pinner.

Reg's formative years were not spent in an atmosphere of domestic bliss. The marriage of Sheila and Stanley Dwight was faltering towards a divorce which was finalized when their only child was in his early teens.

Once a trumpeter in the Bob Miller Band, Stanley Dwight had risen through the ranks of the Royal Air Force. His authoritarian mien extended to the relationship with Reg, who dreaded his homecomings.

'He never let me do anything that I wanted,' the star would later reflect.' I couldn't even play in the garden in case I might damage his rose beds. I was petrified of him.'

At the time his father's frosty countenance was a source of bafflement as much as misery. Reg was a diligent student who was well behaved at home and outside.

Having said that he wanted no further children, Stanley Dwight fathered four in consecutive years after remarrying. The embittered relationship with his first born would latterly be conducted through the channels of the media.

Although even the common denominator of music was a source of conflict in the Dwight household, Reg was, from a toddler, exposed to the 78 r.p.m. sounds of such artists as Frankie Laine, Doris Day, Nat King Cole, Rosemary Clooney, Guy Mitchell and his father's favourite, George Shearing. A few new records were brought into the home every Friday.

The discovery of a natural aptitude for piano playing at a pre-school age can be largely attributed to the forbearance of his grandmother, who allowed the baby Dwight to bang on the piano keys if he became irritable. By the time he was three, Reg found that he could play from memory the record he had just listened to.

Once his mother had introduced him to the dangerous sounds of Elvis, there was no turning back – even if Sheila Dwight baulked when Elton came home with Little Richard's 'She's Got It' and 'The Girl Can't Help It'. 'She liked rock but not Little Richard.'

Music was his conduit for escape whenever the domestic peace was threatened. Pocket money was spent on records, assimilated and catalogued obsessively, and soon after enrolment at Pinner County Grammar School, Reg won a scholarship to the Royal Academy of Music, where he spent 'every Saturday morning playing my Chopin *études* and passing my grade examinations.

'Looking back, I did learn chord structures and how to read music. But at the time I was bloody furious.' Sufficiently so to play truant from classes, managing to keep his absence a secret from his parents by spending the requisite hours in constant motion on the London Underground Circle Line.

Reg's adolescent life proved somewhat happier than his childhood. Although Pinner County Grammar favoured rugby over his beloved football, he played whenever he could in · extra-curriculum hours, arriving in the morning at eight o'clock for a tennis ball kick–around in the playground before lessons. In those Tarmac fixtures, he favoured a position out on the wing.

In addition to playing in an occasional team formed with friends, he is remembered by contemporaries as being one of the first boys at the school to take advantage of its tennis facilities.

He was additionally among the clique who chose to support the local football club rather than journey to the more exotic locations of White Hart Lane or Stamford Bridge.

Masters at the school remember Reg Dwight as the sort of pupil who attracted attention neither for behavioural misdemeanours nor academic excellence, although his tutors had expected him to achieve competent examination passes.

Bill Johnson, Reg's form master in his last days at Pinner Grammar, recalled that the pupil had to suffer the pain of indifference to his music from both his contemporaries and staff, particularly the latter.

Of probable greater hurt was his nickname: 'I won't reveal what it was but it referred to his physical characteristics. He was concerned about his appearance even in those days.'

Bill Johnson contended that Reg's first gig was an interval turn on the Pinner Grammar grand piano during a school dance. Audience reaction was measured rather than ecstatic.

However, classmate Mick Randall recalled him performing 'Great Balls Of Fire' *à la* Jerry Lee Lewis in a first-form revue. It was a similar burst of Jerry Lee antics which, a dozen years later, proved a crucial denominator in the American discovery of Elton John.

Randall dismissed accounts of Reg as a shy, gawky schoolboy. 'I always felt that he possessed a great deal of confidence. He was a good friend with a generous nature who enjoyed a laugh.'

Sitting next to Reg during music periods was an education in itself. 'It was during the Russ Conway era. He would spend the time in the class writing one of those sort of songs and play it at the end of the lesson.'

Although he could impress Mick Randall and others with his comprehensive knowledge of pop, Reg's schoolday fame was the product of exterior events – having a close relative (Roy Dwight) playing in the Football League's highest sphere for Nottingham Forest.

Back at the household of the Pinner Dwights, there was no easing of the petty paternal restrictions imposed by father on son. The list of proscribed sartorial items even extended to Hush Puppies – hardly the most outrageous brand of footwear.

Fat, and confessing to a massive inferiority complex, Reg could then hardly have dreamed of avenging such deprivations through stage costumes sufficiently exotic to make Liberace blanch. If he seemed confident enough at school, other social situations filled him with dread: 'If I walked into a room I would clam up.'

Miming to rock records and day-dreaming about being a star was the only way Reg could instil self-confidence.

It was typical of Stanley Dwight's contradictory attitudes towards his son that he was against Reg's pursuance of a musical career.

An often quoted letter from the erstwhile band member urged Reg to jettison his musical ambitions in favour of a respectable job with Barclays Bank or BEA, the national airline.

But Sheila – who had always rallied to her son's defence in family disputes – gave him her full support. This extended to Reg's obligatory phase in a schoolboy band with Stuart Brown, who would remain a central character in his early professional life.

Unsurprisingly, Reg continued to live with his mother after the divorce. Schoolfriends recall him maintaining a discreet silence about his home life, confiding only that his father was regularly away. Few were invited inside the Dwight household.

The Beatles, a seminal influence, made their chart début with 'Love Me Do' when Reg was a fourth-former.

He was captivated by the haircuts and jackets, but, primarily, by the songs. To this day, he maintains that in terms of quality and quantity, John Lennon and Paul McCartney stand head and shoulders above all other vaunted twentieth-century songwriting permutations.

Determined to carve out a life for himself in any branch of the music industry, Reg left school before A-levels to take a job as messenger at the publishing company, Mills Music, much to the chagrin of his music teacher, Bill Stoupe.

Bill Johnson considered the relationship Reg enjoyed with the music master to have not been without its friction – largely through Stoupe's wariness of the pop idiom.

'Bill Stoupe approved of Reg's initiative and that his playing showed a sound technical base. He just thought it was a great pity that his talent should be put to use in the way it was.'

However, on learning that Reg was eschewing an academic career in favour of a job of bottom-rung eminence, Bill Johnson offered the pupil sanguine guidance: 'You may end up as a glorified office boy . . . or a millionaire.'

Within the school, minimal opposition was expressed to the departure of the new A-level student. 'It was generally accepted that to succeed in the pop business, as Reg obviously wanted to, it was going to be necessary to start in that sort of job.'

Before leaving Pinner Grammar, however, he did figure significantly in a major political event – standing as the Tory candidate in a mock election. History does not recall whether the candidacy was coveted or coerced. Nor is the result documented.

In terms of his duties – commuting between the company and the post office with self-packed parcels – the job at Mills Music lived down to its description. Yet Reg enjoyed even this peripheral involvement in the business, in the process coming into contact with people who would later influence his career. For example, young songwriters, Roger Greenaway and Roger Cook, then at Mills and about to establish themselves with a top-three record for the Fortunes, 'You've Got Your Troubles'.

Outside office hours, he would substantially increase his income with performances of standard melodies at the Northwood Hills Hotel, a short drive from his home.

The term 'hotel' is something of a misnomer. It was a public house which, at intervals, had taken in paying guests. Today, it is known as the Northwood Hills.

One imagines, nonetheless, that it required great courage for the self-effacing sixteen-year-old to approach landlord, George Hill, for a job.

'He said he wanted to play piano in the pub,' Hill reminisced. 'My last pianist could no longer take the travelling so I said I'd give him a trial before the customers and see how he did.' Having passed this public audition, Reg entertained the punters on a regular basis.

The Dwight repertoire was a catholic one. George Hill remembered 'pub standards, singalong stuff, his own songs – he was writing in those days – and a lot of rock. He would start at seven and play until closing time at ten thirty.'

Remuneration was the princely sum of £1 a night, multiplied many times over by the donations of the Northwood Hills clientele. 'One of my customers, Toby, used to take a tin tray round for a collection.'

George Hill can quite believe the star's later assertion that he ended up with £25 a week. 'A generous lot, the people here.'

Despite being 'a shy and nervous young man', there was evidence of future crowd-pulling potential.

'Reg certainly brought in trade – 150 people were here on a good night. 'According to George Hill, Reg had two constant fans in his entourage. 'His mother and, I believe, his future stepfather (Fred Farebrother) came to help him set up his equipment.'

Basically, this entailed the amplifier which didn't endear him to all the Northwood Hills regulars.

'The older people couldn't stand his music. Some would threaten to pull the wires out of his amplifier. Some would actually do it.'

On the less appreciative nights, Reg would grit his teeth and think of the money he was making, totalling enough to purchase an electric piano and amp.

While the punters may have infinitely preferred the singalong standards to original Dwight compositions, the Hills allowed him to rehearse his own material in the pub on Sunday afternoons. The piano, no longer in use, today carries authenticated proof of its prime part in the launch of a star as it awaits a possible auction.

A scrawled note on headed Watford Football Club notepaper declares: 'This is to certify that this piano has played many a wrong note, only due to me. Long live pub uprights (and the Northwood Hills).'

The landmark engagement remains acknowledged in the star's *Who's Who* entry.

In the Merseybeat era, the prospects for a portly, bespectacled piano player were not the stuff of dreams. The Beatles were conquering America like no British act before or since, leaving Gerry and the Pacemakers, Billy J. Kramer and other conveyor-belt discoveries to prosper on the domestic market. If you wanted pathos, there was Freddie and the Dreamers.

It was the Rolling Stones who gave hope to the less than perfectly formed aspirants. Mick Jagger didn't want to hold his lady's hand if they could spend the night together. In stark contrast to many other bands, the Stones had no need to articulate a debt to the blues legends. The music spoke volumes.

The increasing eminence of blues-based bands coincided with the formation of Bluesology, featuring one Reginald Dwight on electric piano. A bassist, drummer and guitar vocalist – respectively Rex Bishop, Mick Inkpen and the previously mentioned Stuart Brown – completed the original line-up. Although initially favouring material from the burgeoning Tamla Motown and Stax soul collections, the band – playing semi-professionally around the London area – graduated to material by Jimmy Witherspoon and other artists who were then little known.

Chartbound Bluesology were not. Yet having resigned his residency at the Northwood Hills Hotel as the band's bookings increased, Reg garnered invaluable experience as Bluesology supported touring American stars – among them Major Lance and Patti Labelle, who, as a card-sharp, remembered taking money off the unworldly pianist, assuaging her guilt through a stint in the kitchen.

The nearest Bluesology came to the Beatles' path to glory was a stint at the Top Ten Club in Hamburg, though they did play the venues that were then the staple of the London R. & B. circuit – clubs with evocative names like the Cromwellian and the Bag O'Nails.

Reg Dwight's role in the band remained as one of the supporting cast. His musical ambition expanded in correlation to his girth, but progress was slow. Encapsulating the title of a future LP, *Don't Shoot Me I'm Only The Piano Player*.

He was, in fact, the vocalist on the first of a trio of commercially disastrous Bluesology singles, 'Come Back Baby', which he also wrote, albeit because the song was beyond the range of front man, Stuart

Brown. But in the tradition of band politics, 'Come Back Baby' was not included in Bluesology's stage act.

Enter Long John Baldry.

Baldry – the Long John acknowledged a great height (6 feet 7 inches) – was in the vanguard of the development of British rhythm and blues. His rasping voice was featured in Alexis Korner's Blues Incorporated and later with Cyril Davies. When Davies died in 1964, Baldry had inherited his band, retitled it the Hoochie Coochie Men and recruited a youthful Rod Stewart as second vocalist.

When the singer found himself back on his own, Bluesology were offered the chance to be Baldry's full-time backing band. Impressed by his status and the prospect of reasonable remuneration – at least £15 a week each at a time when 25 pence a night could buy bread and breakfast in northern lodgings – the offer was taken up. The result was an altered line-up, eventually incorporating a brass section and girl singers, and an extensive touring schedule. Certainly, the boss man perceived no great future for the least extrovert of his supporting cast, noticeable mainly for having the most equipment in the band.

'Nobody expected Reg to become anything big,' Baldry later confessed. 'He was a shy person, almost introverted on stage.' Nor was he the life and soul of the party.

Baldry remembered that in an attempt to counteract his weight problem, Reg had gone on a special diet, abetted by slimming pills. But a side affect of the medication was a tendency towards petulant aggression. 'I never had rows with him,' Baldry joked. 'But I can't say the same about the rest of the band.'

Reg continued to write songs throughout the Bluesology period which gave no inkling of a substantive future talent.

The beginning of a disenchanting end for him and other band members was the elusive hit single which Baldry had long sought. 'Let The Heartaches Begin', a schmaltzy ballad, entered the charts in November 1967 and reached number one during a thirteen-week residence. At the time, Bluesology boasted its most talented formation, including bassist, Freddy Gandy, drummer, Pete Gavin, and backing vocalist, Marsha Hunt, who went on to achieve a measure of notoriety on and off stage.

Thereafter, Baldry's career, and reputation, plummeted as he took Bluesology into what its famous pianist would later dismiss as the 'fish and chip' ambience of the cabaret circuit.

One by one, the defections came, opinion being divided as to whether some were sackings for reason of economy. Reg was not the first to depart – Marsha Hunt was among those who preceded him – but he did have a career alternative.

A few months earlier, he had taken the initiative of replying to an advertisement placed by Liberty Records in *New Musical Express* for new talent – 'artists/composers; singer-musicians to form new group'. The ad was the idea of the label's youthful head of A. & R., Ray Williams, who 'at the ripe old age of eighteen decided that the quickest way to find artists was to organize some kind of talent search.'

With hindsight, the hundreds of replies the advertisement elicited can be seen to have included a disparate collection of future stars.

Among the respondents were the zany Bonzo Dog Doo Dah Band, Martin Barre of Jethro Tull, Mike Batt of Wombles infamy and Jeff Lynne of ELO, who was then in the fêted underground band, Idle Race.

Reg was invited to attend an audition, recalled with affection by Ray Williams. Because of his limited singing experience with Bluesology, he reverted to songs like Jim Reeves' 'I Love You Because' and 'He'll Have To Go', which had been the cornerstone of his pub programme at the Northwood Hills. Under the circumstances, it was hardly surprising that Liberty decided to pass up on the chance of signing this particular untried talent.

'I felt quite sympathetic towards him,' said Ray Williams. 'He told me he was lost in Bluesology because Baldry wouldn't let him sing. Yet there was something unique about his voice – it was odd and it was interesting.' Admitting to Ray Williams that lyrics were not his forte, Reg was rewarded with the information that a lyricist from Lincoln-shire three years his junior had submitted some work. Would he be interested in seeing it?

The lyricist was one Bernie Taupin, whose mother had also exhibited a crucial influence on his career path. Bernie's young life had already been interspersed with nomadic interludes. It was his poetry – 'all psychedelic "canyons of your mind" stuff' – which had inspired the response to the NME ad. But for whatever diffident reasoning, the letter was consigned to the rubbish bin . . . 'My mother found it in the waste basket and posted it.'

Reg was impressed by the images conjured up by the lyrics and immediately put a melody to some of Bernie's words. Reference to that first song, 'Scarecrow', was made eight years later on the auto-biographical *Captain Fantastic* album, by which time the writing partnership was as well known as those of Lennon and McCartney and

Jagger and Richard. In 1967, Ray Williams was the only receptive audience.

It was not through lack of effort on the part of Williams that Liberty didn't put the duo on the payroll. Undeterred, he tried another explorative avenue.

'At that time a friend of mine was Graham Nash of the Hollies, who had a company called Gralto (with the other writers in the group, Allan Clarke and Tony Hicks). We set up this little arrangement for some promising writers that Liberty didn't want to sign.'

Ray Williams himself set up a company, Niraki, with associates Nicky James and Kirk Duncan. 'Any talent that came from us would go through Gralto and in turn be administered by the Dick James organization. That's how Reg and Bernie got started.'

Dick James has been rather unkindly described as 'not the man who made the Beatles – rather one of the many men the Beatles made'. It was either an inspired or fortuitous decision by James not to turn Brian Epstein down when he walked into his office with a demo of 'Please, Please Me', which had been rejected by practically every other publishing company. In 1963, he and Epstein set up the Beatles' publishing company, Northern Songs. The rest, as they say, is history.

James was not immediately privy to the potential of the Dwight–Taupin collaboration. Although the songwriting partnership was an impersonal one – the two corresponded entirely by mail for the first six months – Reg was industriously putting music to the lyrics his postman delivered at the four-track DJM studio in New Oxford Street, in the heart of the West End.

While he was still fulfilling Bluesology commitments, his involvement in the group was nearing its conclusion, to great personal relief.

In the formative days Reg had been aghast at the band's lack of ambition, even though it was being booked by the big London clubs. In the latter period, frustration stemmed from Baldry's musical regression.

However, Bluesology did leave one lasting career imprint – the name of Elton John. John was as in Baldry; Elton was taken from Bluesology's sax player, Elton Dean, whose lesser claim to fame was through stints in Soft Machine and the Keith Tippett Group.

The name was later altered officially by deed poll, with the addition of the middle name of Hercules. He explained: 'I wanted to change it legally because it was such a hassle having two names, like leading two lives. I used to have the middle name Kenneth which is so useless. No one ever called me Kenneth – I don't know why people bother having middle names anyway. So I thought I'd call myself Hercules. My mother had a fit. Everybody had a fit. They didn't think I was serious until it came to it.'

In truth, the new improved title would have counted for little had not an old acquaintance been in a position of semi-authority at Dick James' small West End studio.

Caleb Quaye was a respected session musician whose life had certain parallels with that of the former Reginald Dwight. Caleb's musical heritage covered four generations. His father was a jazz musician, his mother sang in the same band.

Like Elton, he could play the piano at the age of four and also worked on the periphery of the business as a messenger boy for a competing concern. Dissimilarly, he had mastered the guitar, being engaged for his first session work at the age of sixteen.

Well before Elton and Bernie had established face-to-face contact, Caleb was engineering the demos of the formative John–Taupin collection.

As Bernie admitted, the period threw up no undiscovered classics. 'At that time I was writing some very banal stuff and Reg was writing straight commercial pop tunes.'

With considerable embarrassment, the lyricist recalled writing a number called 'Swan Queen Of Laughing Lake' in 1967. 'It had every cliché in the book.'

The relationship took on a more personal touch when Bernie, with great reluctance, finally began venturing to London and the Dick James studio. A scion of the country, whose remunerated employment had largely consisted of labouring jobs on farms, his rustic outlook on life was the antithesis of Elton's regard for occupational and financial stability.

Nevertheless, it was a case of opposites attracting as the two got on as well in the studio as they did by correspondence.

Their incipient partnership was abetted by the indulgence of Caleb Quaye, who, whether through prescience or friendship, allowed them to keep on making demos while leaving Dick James in blissful ignorance of the arrangement. In fact, comparable generosity was shown to others, until the inevitable happened.

Office manager, Ronnie Brohn, happened to pass the building at ten o'clock one evening and was surprised to see the lights on, no studio time having been booked to his knowledge. As the premises were situated above a branch of the Midland Bank, senior employees were aware of the need for vigilance in security matters. Brohn decided to investigate and discovered Caleb, Elton and some others at work on illicit recordings.

His outrage stoked by a dislike of Caleb, Brohn stormed into the office of studio manager, Stephen James (Dick's son), the following morning to inquire as to whether the motley nightshift crew had authorization to be there. Stephen James replied in the negative and summoned a belligerently contrite Caleb Quaye, who eventually admitted that Elton and company had been utilizing studio time and equipment to lay down demos of their own.

James asked to hear the tapes, which he found of sufficient interest to take to his father.

It is open to debate whether the former crooner with the Henry Hall and Geraldo bands discerned any great potential in what he heard. But influenced by the encouraging opinions of others within the organization, Dick James signed up the John–Taupin partnership on a songwriting contract at £25 a week, of which Elton received the major share. Their brief was to come up with material suitable for the likes of Tom Jones and Cilla Black. It was a start.

Ray Williams's recall of the period depicts Dick James in a less benevolent light. 'What happened in reality,' he alleged, 'was that Dick James stole them not only from us (Niraki) but from Gralto.' But with their careers going nowhere, it did not seem as though they had much alternative. Once aware of Dick James's interest, Elton was keen to break with Gralto anyway.

Apprised of the new arrangement, the controlling Hollies were said to be not unhappy, provided that Gralto could keep the songs written by the duo while in its employ.

A change of company did not immediately herald a change in fortune. Elton – whose vocalist experience with Bluesology had been minimal – was back on record through a tie-up with Philips. The result was a single, 'I've Been Loving You', advertised as 'the greatest performance on a first disc' by '1968's great new talent'. More apposite was the rider: 'You have been warned.'

The great new talent was not about to usurp the cutesy Israeli duo of Esther and Abi Ofarim as the label's top sellers. The record sunk without trace.

Another false dawn (and retrospective godsend) was the selection of a John–Taupin composition, 'I Can't Go On Living Without You', as a prospective British Eurovision entry. One of the better manifestations of public taste saw it finish way below 'Boom Bang-A-Bang' in the qualifying final in the year Lulu represented Britain.

At least, Elton had the good grace to admit culpability for the lyrics, explaining that they illustrated why he normally put music to Bernie's words.

I n later days, Elton and Bernie would cringe at the banality of some of their earliest compositions. 'The first things we did weren't very good at all,' Bernie recalled. 'Our hearts just weren't in them.'

Cilla Black recorded a version of the failed Eurovision entry; Edward Woodward demonstrated why his fame lay in his acting abilities by covering the duo's 'Tide Will Turn For Rebecca', described by Elton as 'a real John Hanson number'.

Of possibly greater obscurity was 'The Flowers Will Never Die', recorded by Ayshea, whose marginal claim to fame was hosting a pop show for children. Song, and singer, reached the final of the Yamaha Song Festival in Japan but didn't win. Now not a lot of people know that.

A financial killing may be made someday by the entrepreneurial soul who locates, then takes a chance with a never released promotional album which reflected Bernie's obsession with psychedelia. Titles like 'Regimental Sergeant Zippo' must have transported Elton back to the dawn of Flower Power, when Long John Baldry instructed him to go out and purchase the requisite kaftan and trappings. An album of its era, it is remembered by the singer with acute embarrassment.

The drummer on the recordings was Roger Pope, who was to maintain an intermittent working relationship with Elton over the next decade. Like bassist, Tony Murray, he went on to play on the first LP.

It took a new ally within the Dick James set-up to recognize the potential inherent in what, hitherto, had been viewed as the average songwriting team of John and Taupin.

Steve Brown, recruited to the company as a song plugger, told the partnership in forthright terms that its material was not up to scratch. It was Brown's belief that Elton and Bernie were failing through attempting to reconcile their own tastes with those of Dick James.

Bernie vividly recalled the lecture. 'When Steve told us that our stuff was terrible, and that we weren't doing what we could, we were really down and depressed. But I realized that he was right – we had to write for ourselves. So we went away and came back with "Lady Samantha".'

Holding a position ascendant to Caleb Quaye, Steve Brown inherited the role of chief supporter of the duo before Dick James. Lionel Conway, head of DJM's music publishing, also gave encouragement and it did the partnership's cause no harm that on a selling mission, Stephen James was told by a producer that while the John–Taupin songs were too individual for other artists, the voice on the demos (Elton's) displayed promise. Had the company considered having him record the songs? The demos contained most of the material which appeared on the first Elton John album.

Once Dick James had been convinced of the wisdom of the idea, the question then arose as to who was to take charge of the sessions. Although without prior production experience – his chief musical accomplishment was as sax player with Emile Ford and the Checkmates – Steve Brown coerced James into letting him produce 'Lady Samantha' as a possible single. With the company's studio being used for the session, there was nothing to lose from the experiment.

Recorded in an evening, the end product initially disheartened the protoganist. However, on the single's release in early 1969, the critics raved . . . well almost. 'Nice, though it's much as we've heard before' (*Disc*). 'Lyrics are sensible and worthwhile – a promising talent' (*New Musical Express*). 'An interesting guitar-ridden sound that could well create waves of interest' (*Melody Maker*).

The single went on to become a hit in terms of airplay, winning many a disc-jockey's seal of approval. None the less, sales were nothing to write home about.

And if the vocals carried greater conviction than the lyrics, no matter. Reggie Dwight was dead. Long live Elton John.

The breakthrough of sorts achieved by 'Lady Samantha' persuaded Dick James to consent to Elton recording an album of the kind of songs that he and Bernie could take pride in.

The album was titled *Empty Sky*, recorded in the early months of the year at the DJM studios, with Steve Brown again in charge of the production. The main personnel were as for the single – Caleb Quaye, on guitar, Tony Murray, on bass, and Roger Pope, on drums. Additional instrumentation ran to saxophone, flute and harmonica.

A future portent was the percussive appearance on 'Lady What's Tomorrow' of Nigel Olsson.

'I can remember more about making *Empty Sky* than later albums,' Elton recalled. 'It's such a great feeling to be able to make a record. The first one is never the best but always the most memorable.'

In a belated review, he selected 'Hymn 2000' as a prime example of the LP's pretentious leanings.

Contrastingly, a track exhibiting genuine promise was 'Skyline Pigeon', an evocative ballad which set the pattern for 'Your Song'.

That 'Skyline Pigeon' was published by Cookaway Music is testimony to the crucial interest shown by two other believers in the talents of Elton and Bernie within the Dick James organization.

In common with 'Reg who did the parcels' at Mills Music, the Rogers Cook and Greenaway had also transferred allegiance to DJM.

Recalled Roger Greenaway: 'We were impressed by the songs that Elton and Bernie were turning out. I know that Graham Nash really admired their work. But they were both raw and green about the business. They didn't know what was happening. They felt they were getting nowhere.'

Cook and Greenaway had seen the potential inherent in the partnership and were particularly interested in two songs, one of which was 'Skyline Pigeon'. Consequently, the two Rogers went to see Dick James, telling him: 'If we cut any of their material, we want them for Cookaway.'

As Roger Greenaway ruefully reflected: 'I'm sure that Dick James took a greater interest because of our enthusiasm. Yet bearing in mind the Beatles thing, it was nice to be around when lightning did actually strike twice in the same place.'

Empty Sky was released on DJM, Elton now having signed up with the fledgling label of the Dick James organization. The reality was that there was little option.

While 'Lady Samantha' had come out on Philips, it was made abundantly clear that the company had no desire to go with an LP in advance of a hit single. A blazing row ensued between Stephen James and Philips' A. & R. man, who when asked to tear up the contract, did.

Costing an estimated £4,000, the initial sales of around 2,500 hardly suggested a megastar in the making. Nor for that matter did the first DJM single, 'It's Me That You Need', a sentiment unreciprocated by the record-buying public. The song did latterly reach a wider audience, being coupled with 'Lady Samantha' on the B-side of 'Honky Cat' in 1972.

Considering the limited impact of his early records, it was no surprise that the realist in Elton had recognized the desirability of supplementing his income, where feasible.

Already displaying the symptoms of a hopeless vinyl junkie, he was in his element working behind the counter in a record store – Musicland in Berwick Street in London's Soho district. Customers' selections fascinated him, regardless of the limited demand for *Empty Sky*.

In the studio, one of his session assignments contributed to a single which proved more enticing to the record shop's clientele. Elton was the uncredited pianist on the Hollies' 'He Ain't Heavy (He's My Brother)', which reached number three in the charts at the end of 1969. Perhaps it was this absence of acknowledgement which prompted Elton's later remark: 'They thought they were making art; I was just having a good time.' A later reputed credit was as backing vocalist on Tom Jones's 'Daughter Of Darkness'.

Other work included the industry's shrine to anonymity – budget-priced LPs and EPs featuring hits of the moment covered by session musicians in the style of the original artists. In the days before multi-star collections, such copy-cat compilations sold handsomely. Music for Pleasure, Avenue and Marble Arch (the budget arm of Pye), were labels which capitalized on Elton's talent for mimicry.

A passable rendition of Stevie Wonder on 'Signed, Sealed, Delivered I'm Yours' was a contemporary personal favourite, bringing wistful reminiscence of the night Wonder had sat in on his Vox Continental during the Bluesology era. Elton also performed the original demos for some saccharine-coated singles, an example being the Brotherhood of Man's 'United We Stand'.

If his musical future was a sizeable question mark at this point, his private life was a painful echo. Though never completely at ease in the metropolis, Bernie had joined Elton in a rented flat in Islington after a spell as a house guest of Sheila Dwight.

Also residing at the flat was Linda, Elton's girlfriend, who he had met at a Long John Baldry Christmas bash. The longer the relationship progressed, the more miserable Elton said he became, claiming that Linda hated his music.

The relationship was progressing inexorably towards marriage. His mother and Bernie were appalled, but displaying perversity in adversity, the groom-to-be held steadfast.

Then, according to Elton: 'The wedding was in two weeks' time and

Long John Baldry was to be best man. Out of the blue he said to me: "Why are you getting married?"

'I respected his opinion because he had no reason to tell me I was wrong, other than he liked me. So I went home at four in the morning and told her the wedding was off.'

Elton's professed reaction to the traumatic experience was a suicide attempt, later acknowledged as a cry for help, rather than a serious bid to take his life.

'It was a very Woody Allen-type suicide. I turned on the gas and left all the windows open.'

Though *Empty Sky* earned more in credibility than sales, a generally favourable press may have helped persuade Dick James to demonstrate his faith in Elton the artist by giving him and Bernie free rein to chart a more ambitious course.

By virtue of their quickfire writing, several albums' worth of songs were awaiting the production stage. Candidly, Steve Brown admitted that the sophisticated orchestral production the songs required necessitated more expert hands behind the controls.

An attempt to engage the Beatles' producer, George Martin, having run aground, the choices of Elton and Bernie were Gus Dudgeon and Paul Buckmaster, producer and arranger respectively on David Bowie's 'Space Oddity', one of the most technically ambitious records of the era.

The first recruit was Buckmaster, the product of a classical background. With a pianist mother, his musical interest was nurtured to the extent that he was playing the cello at the age of six and spent two years in his early teens at the Naples Conservatoire.

Buckmaster in turn recommended Dudgeon, whose early production assignments had been for the diverse triumvirate of the Strawbs, Michael Chapman and the Bonzo Dog Doo Dah Band.

Lukewarm at first about Elton and Bernie's material Dudgeon found that familiarity bred content and decided to accept the project. The best songs were divided into candidates for the two albums released in 1970 – *Elton John* and *Tumbleweed Connection*.

Of the *Empty Sky* personnel, old friend, Caleb Quaye remained a studio regular. Roger Pope was featured to a lesser extent, as were bassist, Dave Glover and Ian Duck. The quartet named above were soon to resurface as Hookfoot.

The use of top session musicians Herbie Flowers and Barry Morgan could equally be viewed as something of a family connection, as both were involved with Blue Mink, a chart band whose joint lead vocalist was staunch Elton believer, Roger Cook.

Both the new LPs were planned in meticulous detail. Considering the use of orchestra, an outlay of £6,500 (Dick James's own figures) on the *Elton John* album seems outrageous value for money. Nevertheless, a total of fifty-five hours of recording time was evaluated by James as 'very high for a new artist' in 1969–70.

With enriched hindsight, the company chief later averred: 'But we all felt he was worth it.'

For the eponymous LP, the DJM studios had been forsaken for the more advanced facilities available at another London studio, Trident, where engineer, Robin Cable, could be counted as a fan. 'For me,' said Elton, 'a studio has to be moody and a bit cosy and Trident's like that.' For Paul Buckmaster's orchestrations, 'the marvellous string sounds' the studio could produce was a crucial selling point.

So happy was the artist with the Trident set-up that he declined an offer to record at The Band's own studio in Upstate New York.

To the casual follower of early 1970s music, the *Elton John* album will be remembered for one of the most enduring popular singles of the period – the touchingly simplistic 'Your Song'.

Diehards still consider the collection hard to surpass. The soulful 'Border Song' depicts Elton at the peak of his balladry powers. Proof of the song's potency came when it was later covered by Aretha Franklin, queen of soul in the eyes of Elton and the world.

The vocals on 'No Shoestrings On Louise' suggest the influence of Mick Jagger, a confessed idol of the singer, while 'Take Me To The Pilot' turned up the power to the mid-point level where Elton appeared most comfortable.

The artist later admitted that 'Take Me To The Pilot' – and 'The Cage' – reflected Bernie's interest in science fiction, adding the confession that he'd experienced difficulty in identifying with lyrics he found unintelligible.

When the album was released in the spring of 1970, the sales were only marginally more encouraging than those of *Empty Sky*. It took Elton's unprecedented reception in America five months later to revive home interest.

If Elton John was Bernie's sci-fi LP, *Tumbleweed Connection* represented a more long-standing love of his lyricist . . . Americana.

'*Tumbleweed* was something I'd always wanted to do for I have always been interested in the history of the Old West,' Bernie explained. 'In a way I suppose you can say they are cowboy songs.'

The tub-thumping 'Burn Down The Mission' became a staple of

Elton's concert repertoire. 'Country Comfort' was the first Elton song to be covered by Rod Stewart, a fellow football nut and extrovert stage performer who was carving out a solo career in tandem with his frontman role in The Faces.

The LP also included a version of 'Love Song', a tender ballad by Lesley Duncan, the nearest Britain came to a resident Carole King.

Though yet to be extensively showcased on record, the linch-pins of the Elton John Band had by now been recruited.

Bassist, Dee Murray, had served his apprenticeship in the dying embers of the pivotal band of the 1960s, the Spencer Davis Group. Drummer, Nigel Olsson, already had a top-ten hit to his credit, playing on Plastic Penny's 'Everything I Am' in 1968. That short spell in a teeny band had been advantageous. For with the group also being handled through Dick James, he had both been introduced to Elton and worked with him on sessions.

Post-Penny, Olsson joined Murray in Spencer Davis, an acknowledged turning point in his musical life. 'In Dee, I found the first guy I could play alongside. Almost immediately, we knew exactly what we wanted to do, exactly what each other's minds were thinking on stage.' That oneness of purpose was then extended to encompass Elton, by which time a handful of gigs with Uriah Heep had furthered Olsson's experience.

In addition to Olsson's solitary contribution to *Empty Sky*, both he and Murray were also briefly featured on *Tumbleweed Connection*.

The début of the Elton John Band was at the Pop Proms series at the Roundhouse, London, in April 1970 – coinciding with the launch of Paul McCartney's first solo LP and the peak of Simon and Garfunkel's popularity. Headlining the Roundhouse bill were Tyrannosaurus Rex, in the last months before an abridged title (T Rex) and expanded success.

Sandwiched between American assaults, Elton was back at the venue at the end of the year, supporting The Who.

A by-product of his Stateside experiences, no doubt, was a nauseating propensity to give peace signs and 'right on' exclamations. British approval was also noticeably more reserved for the feet on the piano routine that had served him so well before Californian audiences. But the songs took some beating.

At this stage the perseverance with a three-man line-up was vindicated by the reaction of audiences.

'Think of bass, drums and piano and most people will conjure up something that plays in the back room of a pub,' said Dee Murray candidly. 'That's what I used to think. It just goes to show what can be done by putting work into something you believe in.

'It's fantastic how enjoyable it is, amazing what we can do. Often during a set I'll be enjoying it so much that I'll want to have a laugh with Nigel. I'll turn round and take a look at him and he'll be working all over the place. I couldn't imagine how much it's improved our playing, plus the fact that Elton's music contains so much feeling.'

The latter sentiment was echoed by Britain's top DJs. The star names from Radio One voted Elton the most important artist to emerge during 1970.

The station's chief purveyor of progressive rock, John Peel, made *Tumbleweed Connection* his album of the year, while the host of the coveted breakfast show, Tony Blackburn, declared: 'An artist who will be very big once he finds that elusive right song.'

By now, the man without whom there would have been no promising beginnings was back in the professional lives of Elton and Bernie. After keeping abreast of their progress through telephone contact, Ray Williams was invited by Elton to become his manager.

'Now Elton had a contract with Dick James, who was prepared to sell the management agreement if I could come up with enough money,' Williams explained.

'I felt that he was going to make a great deal of money. My idea was to take a percentage, but I wanted a wage as well because, at that point, I could not afford to do otherwise.

'The people I went to for help laughed me out of the room. They said he would have to earn something like 35–40,000 dollars a year to make it worthwhile.'

That really should have put an end to the matter. Only Dick James then decided to make Williams a proposition he was in no position to refuse.

'Dick said to me: "Why don't we do a deal whereby you manage Elton and we'll do it together?" So I ended up managing Elton from Dick James's offices.

'One of the tasks I was responsible for was fixing up Elton's first American tour in 1970.'

How did a podgy, piano-playing singer with a receding hairline manage to endear himself to the American public on a scale hitherto achieved only by those four lovable moptops from Merseyside? Especially when an album highly rated by all at his record company had sold so disappointingly in his homeland.

What should have been an unheralded first visit in the autumn of 1970 became a triumph of inexplicable proportions, given the artist's prior track record.

Credit Dick James for financing the trip at a quoted figure of 10,000 dollars in the wake of the hardly spectacular reaction to Elton's eponymous LP. But would he so readily have defrayed the cost were it not for the wealth of anticipation created by the artist's then American label, UNI? Then again, Elton might not even have boasted a Stateside deal were it not for the fortuitous presence of Roger Greenaway in the office of UNI's Russ Regan the day Lennie Hodes visited him on a selling mission for Dick James Music.

'Lady Samantha' had been put out in the States through a licensing deal with Bell Records. The single had reaped impecunious reward for the company, which, unsurprisingly, declined an option on *Empty Sky*. It was Philips all over again, though in this instance, it took a 500 dollar payment to get Elton off the label.

Now Greenaway had been discussing some songs with Regan when Hodes – who ran the DJM operation in New York – arrived to try and interest UNI in the LP. He was hardly brimming with confidence, having been shown the door by every label he had visited.

'Russ wasn't really sure,' Greenway revealed. 'He liked it but didn't want to commit himself. Elton was an unknown quantity. He hadn't seen him live.

'Now not only was Russ a friend. Roger and I had been very successful in America and he respected my opinion. I told him that if he didn't sign Elton he would miss out on a world star.

'Lennie was amazed and could not wait to phone Dick James with the news.'

Those back in London at the time recall a different scenario. Regan had liked what he heard and had been further swayed by Greenaway's heartfelt appraisal. Yet it was when the UNI executive was sent a tape of the just completed *Elton John* LP that 'he hit the ceiling'.

UNI having been convinced, the company set about alerting the rest of America by way of a little Hollywood-type publicity – like Elton and party being greeted at the airport by a close relative of a London Transport double-decker bus, bearing the slogan, 'Elton John has arrived'. Even by Los Angeles standards, it was not a commonplace sight.

'It was the last thing we wanted,' Ray Williams remembered. 'What was really funny was that they thought they were doing us a favour.'

If the arrival mirrored Elton's sense of the extravagant, the following days surpassed his wildest expectations.

Ecstatic crowds packed out the Troubadour Club in Los Angeles, the press overdosed on superlatives and Bill Graham, probably the most influential American concert promoter of the early 1970s, was quick to engage the artist for his Fillmore venues. The fact that Elton went on to bomb out in San Francisco has been conveniently forgotten in the passage of years. Likewise, retrospective accounts have ignored the profusion of complimentary tickets given away to fill out the venue before word of mouth rendered the action profligate.

Eyes bedazzled with dollar signs, John Maitland, the president of UNI's parent company, MCA, spoke of the Troubadour residency as 'one of the most spectacular openings for an unknown artist I've ever seen'.

Certainly, it did no harm to Elton's image to have Janis Joplin, Dave Crosby, Graham Nash and the Mothers of Invention on the guest list. In a star-conscious society, stellar support was a godsend. Another early convert was multi-instrumentalist, Leon Russell, whose invite home for a jamming session gave Elton more pleasure than the rave reviews. For Russell was also a classically trained pianist who had made his mark in the rock world – in his case live and session work for luminaries like the Stones, Joe Cocker and the Byrds.

Roger Greenaway's recollection was of a small fortune being spent flying in the famous to the Troubadour concerts – 'Neil Diamond was there, as was Quincy Jones.' He also recalled being present when Russ Regan called Dick James, requesting a sum for promotion that way exceeded the record boss's estimate of his financial backing for the tour. Apparently, James assented without hesitation.

Whatever the true outlay, it was money wisely invested. At the end of the Troubadour engagement, Greenaway was listening to his car radio when he heard a disc-jockey preface the arrival of a new rock 'n' roll messiah. To quote a later album title suggestion from Bette Midler, the divine pretender was 'Fat Reg from Pinner'.

There were sceptics back home who dismissed the adulation as a one-off experience. Elton himself was hard pressed to explain his reception, confining his comments to: 'I just got lucky.'

True enough, considering Ray Williams's explanation that the sole reason for selecting the Troubadour was that it offered 150 dollars a week, a previous offer of 50 dollars a week in New York having been laughed off the table.

Given time to reflect, that opening Troubadour gig – 'my night of discovery' – would be assessed by Elton as a character-building experience.

'My career was just getting off the ground in England and it was my first performance in the States. About a thousand people were there, an awful lot of music bigwigs. If I could handle that, I could handle anything.'

At this juncture, the change of name had already justified itself to the artist. 'I'm still the same person as Reg Dwight but Elton John gave me a lot of confidence.'

Conversely, companions on that inaugural visit recall Elton as being anything but self-assured. Ray Williams for one, described him as being extremely nervous, even taking into account that he was under great emotional pressure.

'I remember arguing with him over whether he should do a lunchtime radio show. There was a lot of slamming doors, the beginning of the Elton John we've come to know.'

But the problems went deeper: 'Although, with hindsight, it was probably a mistake, I can remember taking Bernie and everyone else off to Palm Springs with some girls, one of whom was later to be the first Mrs Taupin. We had an amazing time.

'Elton said he didn't want to go. In the end he was lonely and phoned up Dick James, who manipulated the situation for his own ends.' The 'situation' was that, having a duty to be on call at all times, Williams had deserted his post, leaving Elton in a depressed state. On the party's return to London, Williams's managerial role was terminated in, to him, far from satisfactory circumstances.

However, Roger Greenaway believed that Ray Williams was unequal to the task of handling the affairs of an embryonic superstar. 'I don't think he was experienced enough. He just wasn't taking care of business.

'Ray was nowhere to be seen after the Troubadour gigs. He had to go, although considering that he brought Elton and Bernie together, he was treated quite shabbily.'

One who must take much of the kudos for the Stateside break-through was Elton's first American publicist, the imperturbable Norm Winter.

In addition to being the man behind the attention-seeking tour bus, Norm's belief in the artist extended to less than subtle press manipulation.

A *Rolling Stone* reporter was inducted into the sounds of Elton John, having been enticed into the publicist's lair on the pretext of interviewing another band. With the 'interviewees' looking on, Norm disarmed the unsuspecting scribe, by offering to play him something to 'blow your mind. This guy's name is Elton John. We just signed him. I wouldn't try to hype you. I just want your opinion ... Isn't he unbelievable?'

Events proved Norm something of a prophet. Within weeks, Elton was back in the States as a prospective dollar millionaire. While *Tumbleweed Connection* received a welcoming press from UK critics, the Stateside hype was such that it quickly joined the *Elton John* LP in the higher echelons of the US album charts.

So without a British hit single to his name, Elton John entered 1971 as the great white hope of the music world – or in the words of the LA *Times* critic, Robert Hilburn, 'the first rock superstar of the 1970s'.

The irony is that Hilburn typed that licence to print dollars after reviewing a Troubadour night when events deviated from the grand design.

According to the DJM contingent, Elton had become increasingly irate at a palpable lack of attention from the audience, who were paying more attention to nearby conversation than to events on stage.

Finally, Elton's patience snapped. He kicked back the piano stool and screamed: 'If you don't like what I'm playing, maybe it's rock 'n' roll that you want.' The Jerry Lee Lewis antics were brought into play and a star was born.

Nevertheless, Roger Greenaway was adamant that Elton succeeded on his own terms, further declaring that his native country can claim scant credit for his emergence as a global star.

'Nobody can claim that Elton was a British discovery,' he asserted. 'America found him.

'In Britain at that time, image was everything. Elton wasn't good looking but possessed a great amount of talent. He was the guy who broke the mould – and paved the way for later artists like Phil Collins.

'Elton wasn't then into outrageous clothes or other gimmicks. He made it by insisting on doing his own stuff.'

During the second American tour, he had been accorded rock's equivalent accolade to the Papal blessing – Bob Dylan was twice spotted in attendance when Elton played New York's Fillmore East.

Dylan and The Band were among those paying backstage homage to the least obvious eminence-elect since the ageing kiss curl of Bill Haley had prompted the frenzied demolition of cinema seats fifteen years previously.

Paul Simon was another post concert well-wisher.

Further evidence of Elton's rapid rise in America was his being voted top male vocalist in the 1970 *Record World* magazine poll, while he and Bernie were acclaimed best composers in the New York based international music critics awards.

Contrast these to Elton's ninth placing in the British vocal personality category in the same year's *New Musical Express* poll, headed comfortably by Cliff Richard (though he did have the consolation of leading the 'top new disc singer' section, just shading out Dave Edmunds and Robert Plant).

After the depressing latter experiences of Bluesology concerts, Elton was beginning to enjoy live performance once more. 'America did a lot of things for the Elton John band,' he confessed in 1971. 'It made us play a whole lot better. We're now tighter – so tight I can't believe it myself sometimes.'

Confident in himself and his band, there was no diminution in audience rapport as the venues grew larger and his clothes more exotic.

As one who bitterly recalled petty parental restrictions on his teenage wardrobe, his penchant for resplendent stage costumes could be construed as an amalgam of rebellion and showmanship.

Moreover, it could equally be evaluated as reflecting a shrewd understanding of the mechanics of the industry. In later years Elton was able to quote album sales before chart positions and demonstrate his facility around a balance sheet in his capacity as a football club chairman.

The shaded glasses – of inexorably grandiose construction towards the middle of the decade – remedied poor eyesight exacerbated by attempts to emulate the Buddy Holly look.

While comparatively reserved back on that first US tour, he had a product to promote in the ancestral base of the singer–songwriter fraternity. Confounding expectation was as effective a method as any.

'The *Elton John* album has me looking a very dark face on a dark cover,' he later explained. 'People thought that I was gonna come out dressed, well something like Randy Newman – someone very sombre, because some of the tracks were sombre. But I came on and in these clothes played rock 'n' roll, jumped on the piano and just enjoyed it.'

On a different occasion, Elton was to claim a schizophrenic personality, the extrovert side of which only came out on stage. 'It's like that with most performers,' he added. 'Maybe we've all had repressive childhoods.'

For sartorial splendour, his halcyon days were yet to come, with poultry a firm favourite. A massive audience in New York's Central Park in 1980 were treated to their hero attired as a duck – complete with webbed feet. Elton himself expressed a preference for the giant chicken costume which enabled him to out-Muppet the Muppets.

Yet even in the days before his concert ensemble had him resembling the protagonist in a Walt Disney nightmare, the theatricality of Elton's stage shows had not passed unnoticed in the film capital of the world. Paramount at one time thought him the ideal male lead for the Hal Ashby black comedy, *Harold and Maude*, depicting the love affair of a young man fixated with death and an eighty-year-old woman.

In later years, his name would be also touted in connection with a projected movie version of the hit Broadway show, *Candide*. In fact, though a film documentary was made of his Soviet tour in 1979 (*From Russia With Elton*), his only acting credit to date was as the Pinball Wizard in Ken Russell's suitably garish interpretation of Pete Townshend's celebrated rock opera, *Tommy*. It took the video age to confirm Elton's ease in front of the camera.

In comparison with Elton's heady progress towards rock 'n' roll deity across the Atlantic, home achievements had been more measured than meteoric. So when 'Your Song' was released as a single at the

beginning of 1971, reviewers tempered their enthusiasm with recollections of the close encounters of 'Lady Samantha' and 'Border Song'.
Another single from the Elton John album, 'Rock And Roll Madonna',
'sold about two copies in Edgware'.

The choice of singles was to become a perennial source of conflict
between Elton and DJM, and latterly with John Reid.

In 1970, he was content to let others make the mistakes. 'Border
Song' had been a misplaced Steve Brown hunch. 'Rock And Roll
Madonna' was a flawed decision by the James contingent.

Almost imperceptibly, the tide began to turn in favour of the third-
placed selection.

'Your Song' gathered impetus through radio plays as an album track.
Domestic interest increased after the record had reached the American
top ten on the back of his Stateside conquest.

The unlikely catalyst was Tony Blackburn, then the most influential
DJ in Britain.

A solitary play elicited an avalanche of listeners' letters, asking for
details about the singer, track and where they could purchase it.

Blackburn relayed news of the response to Stephen James, with the
rider that, in his opinion, the record was a certain hit. If DJM would
release 'Your Song' as a single, he would make it his record of the week.

The track was put out in single form, Blackburn was as good as his
word and sales justified the optimism.

To the relief of all, and especially DJM, Elton finally had a top ten hit
with the record many diehard fans still rate as his best.

According to Bernie Taupin, the sentiments were those of 'someone
who hadn't written a song before and didn't know how to write. Though
it's a basic love song, it's not supposed to be naive.' The lyrics were
conceived over a romantic plate of bacon and eggs in Pinner and,
contended the writer, did not reflect a personal experience.

The belated home hit may have helped to assuage Elton's pain over
a highly distressing appearance at Midem, the gathering of the
industry potentates at Cannes.

Due to the insensitivity of Eric Burdon, who way exceeded his time
allotment at the first Midem gala concert, and a rogue stage curtain at
the second, Elton's putative showcase turned into a disaster.

Burdon, now representing America with his group, War, blasted
away for over an hour, ignoring the plaintive instructions of the
organizers and precluding Elton's intented closing slot.

When the stage curtain descended upon an unsuspecting Elton

during the second house, the suggestion was that the promoters were out to ensure against a repetition of Burdon's unrequested overtime.

The British representative's only consolation was a PA broadcast of some frank opinions about the event's organization as the audience made for the exits.

At this early stage, Elton's bosses were already worrying that he was taking too much on himself. Concerned about Elton's health, Dick James echoed a physician's warning for him to slow down. There was minimal indication of a positive response.

Within two months of the Cannes débâcle, Elton was on stage in London for his most ambitious yet concert. For 40 pence a seat in the gods, fans saw Elton play half the concert at London's prestigious Royal Festival Hall with his band, returning after the interval with full orchestra, culled from the ranks of the Royal Philharmonic.

The seriousness Elton accorded the occasion was not, he felt, reciprocated by the orchestra, whose members apparently considered that working with a mere pop star did not justify optimum performance.

'I thought they gave a quarter of their best,' commented an aggrieved Elton. 'I felt so tense because I was uncomfortable playing with them.'

Having previously talked about working with an orchestra in America, the RFH experience persuaded him otherwise.

In the US Elton could still do no wrong. Headlining a bill also featuring Seatrain and Wishbone Ash at the Fillmore East, he was rapturously received. Even Bernie was the subject of some generous press for his proficiency on the maracas.

Contrast this with Elton's performance at his major summer gig in England – the Garden Party at Crystal Palace. One reviewer harshly referred to the crowd departing in droves during his set. Another predicted that the best of Elton had already been heard.

Furthermore, Elton may have erred in previewing songs from *Madman Across The Water* – and in not leavening the first part of the set with some of the rock standards he cleverly interprets. A parallel disappointment was an advance performance of the *Captain Fantastic* LP at Wembley Stadium in 1975.

For the defence, it could be pointed out that earlier in the year, Elton had pronounced that his career as a performing rock star would be a short one ... eighteen months.

'Does it sound bad saying I want to quit while I'm at the top? I don't mean it arrogantly. It's just that so many artists never see the end. They never know when they've got that long slide ahead of them.

'It seems so bizarre to talk about the band breaking up but it just has to happen. This is me talking about the inevitable.'

An early example of Elton's facility for the capricious, headline-grabbing statement (later retracted), it did seemingly indicate his regret at the lost opportunity of *Harold and Maude*.

'I really want to do films. But it can't just be another case of a pop star trying his hand at acting. To do it properly you've got to work at it full time, devote all your energy to it. That's why I'll have to retire from all this.'

Within the DJM hierarchy, such comments were seen as another symptom of a schizophrenic personality responsible for a plethora of problems.

Maybe underlying concern about the future of the label's prime asset was a factor in the release of two other DJM albums during 1971.

Bernie Taupin's LP was a selection of poetry with Caleb Quaye among the musical accompanists. In later years, the embarrassed lyricist evaded discussion of the record.

Nigel Olsson's solo album utilized the talents of B. J. Cole, Dee Murray and Doris Troy.

Elton, too, was expanding the scope of his musical activities. In a traumatic year, he honoured a production commitment to a central figure in his professional apprenticeship.

Sandwiched between his transatlantic hopping, Elton produced one side of Long John Baldry's *It Ain't Easy*, an LP heralding a partially effective return to the artist's R. & B. base. Rod Stewart was the other producer.

A speedily assembled project, it illustrated the generous nature of the former pub pianist who had laboured nightly out of the limelight on his Vox Continental when Baldry was the star attraction.

'I wanted to do the Baldry thing as soon as I was asked,' Elton confided. 'I just said "yes" right off without even thinking about it.

'Billy Gaff [the manager of both Baldry and Rod Stewart] phoned me in New York and said that John was in a bad way. He didn't know what to do so would I help him out. I think Rod had already said he would do some producing.'

Though the stars' actions could be interpreted as discharging a common debt, Elton insisted that while liking and respecting Baldry, 'we both believe in his talent'.

Elton selected the material, issued instructions as to how the songs should be recorded and played on the sessions. Unquestionably, it was helpful to the novice producer to involve long-standing collaborators, Caleb Quaye, Lesley Duncan and Roger Cook in the project. Elton was especially complimentary of Quaye's guitar playing.

Referring to the dichotomy between the two producers, Elton spoke of his tracks coming across like butter, with Rod's redolent of barbed wire – an accurate summary of their respective public perceptions.

It Ain't Easy did more for the self-esteem of the central characters than for Baldry's bank balance.

A second star-laden vehicle, *Everything Stops For Tea*, failed equally to impress Warner Brothers Records of Baldry's commercial value, although Elton remained convinced that lacklustre promotion had hampered an incipient American breakthrough.

None the less, Elton had learnt some invaluable lessons to store away for future reference. By the end of 1973, he and Clive Franks were a hit-making production partnership.

Three years after joining Bernie Taupin in a songwriting partnership of seemingly limited horizons, Elton John was being tipped to emulate the accomplishments of his early idols, Jerry Lee Lewis and Little Richard – both no mean showmen, and piano players to boot.

It could all have been so different. While in later years, Elton would (or be advised to) feel sufficiently aggrieved about his earnings during the DJM period to take Dick James to court, a major component of the debt of gratitude he acknowledged to James should be for insisting he resisted a proposition likely to have relegated him back to the supporting ranks.

At the outset, it seemed a golden, unexpected opportunity. Guitar legend Jeff Beck wanting to join the Elton John Band!

Half-jokingly concerned about competing with 'a thousand watts of guitar', Elton invited him for an audition, at which Beck gave a restrained performance, giving credence to the possibility of an unlikely alliance.

Eventually, the penny dropped. Far from being part of a merry band, Beck actually wanted to take over, dropping Nigel Olsson in favour of Cozy Powell. Adding insult to injury, the attempted coup apparently extended to Elton touring the States as a member of the Jeff Beck Group.

'Ten per cent of what he was going to earn,' recalled a bemused Elton. 'And the original idea was for him to join our band.'

With Beck's reputation, ten per cent was still big bucks. But the sage Dick James counselled rejection, reasoning that the reaction to the Troubadour opening would lead to Elton commanding that much, and more, before long.

It took just two months for Dick James to be proved correct, qualifying all concerned for the treasure trove.

After the commercial breakthrough achieved by the *Elton John* and

Tumbleweed Connection LPs, Elton's first two album offerings of 1971 essentially marked time.

The album 17. 11. 70 was a live set recorded on that date for WABC Radio in New York. The first record to prominently feature Dee Murray and Nigel Olsson, it was as unsatisfactory as the majority of live LPs.

Prior to its release, a buoyant Elton described the performance from which the album was culled as one of the most exciting up to that time.

'The sound was excellent. We had an audience of about a hundred and got such a buzz that we played for an hour and a half without interruption. They (WABC) stopped the news, commercials, everything, and ran straight through.' With the benefit of hindsight, Elton made a downward revision of the product.

Close on the heels of 17. 11. 70 came the sound-track album for *Friends*, a Paramount picture directed by Lewis Gilbert.

A formula treatment of teenage love on the run, this nondescript movie would have been forgotten were it not for Elton's musical involvement.

In fact, the LP was split between standard sound-track fare and Elton's songs. It was hardly a career pointer, although the title track – later to resurface on a DJM compilation – sold respectably as a single in America, where Elton's progress continued to outstrip his domestic accomplishments. 'The Honey Roll' was the other song to stand out from the debris of a collection whose quality was later encapsulated by Elton's comment that *Friends* was probably the only US gold album for which every copy was returned. 'You can buy it for 50 cents anywhere you go with a hole punched through it.'

Another grievance was its promotion more as an Elton John LP than a film sound-track. Not only did this erroneously give the impression of being the latest studio album. It ignored the film's stars, none of whom, it should be said, went on to set celluloid alight.

Neither album was considered the legitimate follow-up to *Tumbleweed Connection* and there were commercial grounds for their close proximity.

'The *Friends* album should have been released to coincide with the film. But the American company released it to cash in on my name. And we lost a lot to the bootleggers with the live album. The record company went beserk and said they had to get it out, so it was released months early.'

DJM executives had just cause to rue their eagerness in involving the artist in the sound-track project. The idea, prior to 'Your Song', was to afford Elton an additional avenue of breaking the UK market. In the wake of the hit single, it was far more of a hindrance.

Friends was the last album on which Ray Williams exerted managerial influence – 'I put that together with John Gilbert, the son of the director, when everyone else was having problems,' he claimed. Confessedly then oblivious of what passes for ethics in the music business, his fall from favour surprised him, if not others.

On returning from the first American trip, Elton had allegedly told him: 'I don't know whether it's going to work between us as manager and artist. I just want us to be friends.' This suited Ray fine – 'to be honest, I felt the same. It was a good relationship which did not fuse on a business level.'

Naturally, Ray expected that existing contractual arrangements would be honoured for the period covering the *Elton John* LP, *Tumbleweed Connection*, the live album and film sound-track.

Not so. He claimed that Dick James called him into his office and told him: 'I'm tearing up your agreement, here is £500.' Staggered by the audacity of it all, Ray Williams countered that he would not accept.

In his words, Dick James's riposte was to say: 'OK, I'm holding all your money.'

Ray eventually received £1,500 'under great duress. We had created a great deal of money. But under the control of Dick James, it was not going where it should.'

With Elton and Bernie as godparents to his daughter and a track on *Tumbleweed*, 'Amoreena', dedicated to her, Ray Williams might have expected the opportunity of expressing his displeasure to the artist.

He made numerous attempts to contact Elton, but was never connected. This led him to one of two conclusions. That Dick James's staff were instructed not to let Ray speak to Elton. Or that, true to his dislike of confrontation, Elton was well aware of what was going on and had decided to keep clear.

'I didn't even get a gold disc. They all ended up with John Reid.'

Not much older but a lifetime wiser, Ray Williams departed from Elton's camp, discovered Stealers Wheel – with Gerry Rafferty – and enjoyed the vicarious pleasure of his backstage role in some more hit records.

John Reid soon took over Elton's managership and on longevity alone can be adjudged a great achiever.

The business model of the canny Scotsman, John Reid had progressed far in a short timespan.

Raised in a tough school of life in Paisley, near Glasgow, his father was a welder. A student of marine engineering, he quit his course at eighteen and made his way to London.

Initially working in a men's store, the steely resolution later grudgingly acknowledged by his bitterest of enemies was evidenced by his rapid entry into the music business.

Reid was in Los Angeles when Elton made his Troubadour début in his capacity as the British manager of the famous Tamla Motown label – claiming to have gained admittance to the Motown sanctum by convincing EMI that he was twenty-three, rather than nineteen.

An avid Tamla fan, Elton was constantly calling in on Reid at the EMI offices to cadge the latest releases. His friendship with Reid advanced to the stage where Dick James considered the diminutive Scotsman the person most likely to ensure that the label's precious asset fulfilled his contractual obligations.

James had been in a quandary as to how to regulate Elton's attitude towards his professional commitments. Divergent obstacles were created as his mood veered from petulant lethargy to dangerous enthusiasm.

Those in the business who so admired Elton's capacity for gargantuan touring schedules would not have credited the problems DJM had in the formative days.

According to the company, gigs arranged in London and its environs to give him experience and supplement his income were not honoured. On occasion, payment had to be made to the aggrieved promoters to eschew the threat of legal action.

The problems increased in ratio to Elton's advancement. In the words of a past DJM executive: 'It was a matter of which way he woke up in the morning.'

There were phases when he just wanted to shut himself away in a studio – Elton has himself admitted that at the beginning he believed he could achieve commercial acceptance without recourse to gigging. Conversely, were periods of exhibitionism, when he just wanted to be on stage. Taken to extremes, the consequences for his health were deleterious.

With these factors in mind, John Reid was taken on the DJM payroll in 1971 as Elton's personal manager. While the path to his recruitment was latterly recalled very differently by the parties concerned, on one point there was no dispute. John Reid had spotted the inherent potential in his close friend and was determined to manage him.

If Dick James later thought of Reid as a monster, he could only rue his midwife's role at the birth.

Certainly, Reid was a voracious learner and it is easy to believe his claim that instead of sleeping at night, he used to sit up mulling over the small print of contracts. Within two years, his individualistic method of business study had reaped rich dividends. He was independently managing Elton and, in association with others in the star's inner circle, had established Rocket Records.

Meanwhile, Elton was in a period of unquenchable enthusiasm for touring. With studio commitments as far as the eye could see, his partying capabilities had yet to surface.

'I'm not a raver,' he declared in 1971. 'There's an outrageous side of me but my private life is very quiet. I don't mix – only with friends.

'I won't go out to parties after the gigs. I like to go to the hall, play, exhaust myself. Afterwards, I just want to go to sleep (although) I might read for a while.

'I get up the next day and go on to the next place. That's it.'

He was also aware that approaching the release of a fourth studio album, a critical backlash had already gathered momentum. 'It's funny,' he opined. 'Now that I've made it, it's become very hip to put me down.

'When I was nowhere, it was hip to call me a genius. Now the same critics sneer at me. They won't share me with a mass public – the snobbery in rock is amazing.'

Elton was particularly sensitive to negative coverage from the British rock media. He felt, with a measure of justification, that his American accomplishments had not been accorded due recognition.

However, his claims of reportage tantamout to a bitchy vendetta is not borne out by perusal of the leading journals of the era.

Evidencing all the symptoms of star paranoia, Elton said he had gone out of his way to be nice to everyone, only to be kicked in the teeth as a thank you.

Back home after a mini world tour with an itinerary of the USA, Australia and Japan, Elton had been, once again, riding the trail of positive publicity for the new product – *Madman Across The Water*.

For the record, he enthused. Behind the scenes he shared the manifold doubts expressed in the music press and the less public disquiet of those in the hierarchy of his own label. Disappointing sales served to accentuate the pain.

However anguished at the failure of *Madman*, Elton could rationalize to a reporter that the LP's release coincided with the zenith in appeal of singer-songwriters, James Taylor and Cat Stevens. As all three artists attracted a similar market, substantive sales had been lost.

He could further bemoan that *Madman* had been unnecessarily hurried in its recording. In a singularly unproductive year by past and future standards of the John–Taupin partnership, there was no alternative to the batch of songs Elton took into the studio.

'We had written only about eight songs that year and it came to the point where there was nothing to fall back on if we hated one of the tracks.

'Normally, we write about twenty-five songs a year, so you could tell the sort of state we were in.'

The state was of poor physical and mental health aggravated by an overdose of gigging. In consequence, there had been scant opportunity for writing.

As for those dismissive about the lyrics, Elton had a message: 'People still tend to forget that Bernie's not even twenty-one yet. In a lot of ways he's still very childish and immature.'

Elton himself hardly radiated maturity. The relative misfortune of an LP released just a year after his storming of the States had him contemplating retirement. Not that it wasn't feasible. Financially, the proceeds from the American conquest had already set him up quite nicely, thank you.

Madman completed Elton's first musical cycle, much to the relief of those at DJM who evaluated it as his first really self-indulgent album.

From *Empty Sky* onwards, Elton's piano had vied for domination with Paul Buckmaster's strings. A serious tone had pervaded, leavened by signs of Bernie's increasingly romantic preoccupation. After the esoteric imagery of some of Bernie's early lyrics, he was now focussing on everyday conflicts.

Once again, the LP offered no obvious hit tracks, although in America 'Levon' made the top thirty and 'Tiny Dancer' – a salute to Maxine, the first Mrs Taupin – peaked at 41.

In March, Bernie had made an honest woman of the former Miss Siebelman in his home town of Market Rasen, with Elton fulfilling the duties of best man.

Elton later attested to loathing *Madman* to the extent that he could no longer listen to the album. Later still, he was including many of its songs in his concert repertoire.

Meanwhile, he was well aware that the Elton John Band had run its course as a three-piece outfit. Having eschewed the use of a guitarist to augment the piano-bass-drum line-up, he now conceded that the addition was inevitable.

Not only did the original formation place heavy onus on Elton. After four tours of the States, he was conscious of the need for a fresh approach for the next visit. Similarly, Elton considered the time propitious to ring the changes in other areas of stage presentation. The kicking away of the piano stool had regressed from a spontaneous gesture challenging audience preconceptions to an almost pre-determined segment of a live performance.

'Music has become too technical and precise,' he opined at the year's end. 'I think I've been to blame too as far as records are concerned. It's lost that lovely rawness.'

To his mind, the best purveyors of raucous rock on record during the year had been Rod Stewart and Marc Bolan's T. Rex.

The album, *Every Picture Tells A Story*, and single, 'Maggie May', had deservedly catapulted Stewart to international stardom. Bolan's fame was more confined, the product of two British number ones in 'Hot Love' and 'Get It On' and an exceptional long player, *Electric Warrior*.

Elton was on working terms with them both. Stewart, of course, was co-producing Long John Baldry with him. The Bolan liaison was appreciated by the Fairfield Hall, Croydon, audience, during a winter tour of Britain.

The consensus from the stalls was that Elton was nearing the end of his performance when Bolan made a suitably grandiose entrance from the wings, clad in satin with arm aloft to orchestrate the reception.

A concert within a concert ensued as both stars essayed classic rock 'n' roll performing modes – Bolan down on his knees, Elton upwardly mobile in the style of Jerry Lee Lewis.

Outside of such eminent domestic exceptions as Bolan and Stewart, Elton, who at this point rated himself musically more American than British, listed his favourite artists as Neil Young, The Band, Buffalo Springfield, Grateful Dead, Jefferson Airplane and, of course, Leon Russell.

One of the bastions of American culture, New York's Carnegie Hall, had been a prestigious inclusion on his touring schedule for the year.

When Elton returned to the Carnegie in 1972, a new phase in his recording and performing mien had commenced.

D
avey Johnstone was an unlikely selection as the Elton John
Band's guitarist. A blond string bean of Scottish descent, he
certainly looked the part. But his musical credits largely
reflected the musical genre Elton was eager to distance himself from.

A multi-instrumentalist – his credits at the time encompassed guitar, banjo, mandolin and assorted other stringed instruments – Davey had played clubs and pubs accompanying folk act, Noel Murphy, before joining Magna Carta, 'a Pentangley sort of group'. (Pentangle, an amalgam of some of the finest talents in the British folk scene, enjoyed a period of acclaim in the early 1970s.)

Fortuitously, Magna Carta were produced by Gus Dudgeon, so Elton was comprehensively appraised of Davey's abilities. He'd also been playing sessions for those in the vanguard of the folk movement – for example, Julie Felix and Ralph McTell – and had worked with Bernie on his solo LP.

It was largely at the behest of Gus Dudgeon that Davey had been introduced to the set-up on *Madman Across The Water*, for which he contributed to three tracks. His official induction to the Elton John Band was a Royal Festival Hall concert in February 1972.

Illustrating Elton's propensity for changing his mind, the Festival Hall concert re-united him with an orchestra for live performance a year after chastising the Royal Philharmonic Orchestra members who appeared with him at the same venue. On this occasion, the liaison was acknowledged as more productive.

He had also been in France with the other band members working on the album which would resuscitate Elton's commercial and artistic fortunes.

Not that he was out of the news for long. 'Burn Down The Mission' took on an almost literal meaning during a hometown gig at Watford Town Hall. The band was halfway through the song when a police inspector hijacked Elton's piano stool to announce that a caller, claiming to be from the IRA, had warned of a bomb positioned under the stage. One thousand fans were evacuated as police searched the building for twenty minutes.

And in addition to fund-raising concerts realizing over £2,000 for the National Youth Theatre, Elton gave a free performance for NYT members who couldn't afford benefit show prices.

April gave the first indication that the new album would live up to the rumours. A new single, 'Rocket Man', moved John Peel to comment: 'The band is great, the song is great and Bernie Taupin's lyrics are great. If the Honky Chateau LP is going to be like this, you're going to have to listen to it in little doses or you'll go mad.'

Elton's subject charted a less extravagant course than the astronaut in David Bowie's 'Space Oddity' – another Gus Dudgeon production. Rousing and evocative, 'Rocket Man' delivered a polished alternative to the glam and glitter rock populating the British charts. The star was not being jocular when he ascribed the commercial accomplishments of certain bands to a visual image which he had inspired, rather than any discernible musical talent.

'Rocket Man' complemented its title by shooting up the singles listings to number two – still Elton's highest solo placing in his homeland.

On his return to America in April, a little unsubtle promotion helped boost sales of the record. Elton and the band spent four hours touring the NASA premises in Houston in the wake of the splashdown of Apollo 16.

He lunched with Al Worden – the command module pilot of Apollo 15 – and experienced a simulated space flight, perfect in every detail except that his spacecraft ran out of fuel in the mission's final minutes!

Completing the tour in Minneapolis in May, it was back to Britain for a historic 'Top Of The Pops' taping.

Long John Baldry had been invited to perform 'Iko Iko' off his second Elton John and Rod Stewart produced LP, Everything Stops For Tea.

'Iko, Iko' was off Elton's side of the album, so he was keen to do backing vocals. When Rod got to hear of the arrangements he made it clear that he also wanted to be involved. With other band members and Lesley Duncan in attendance, the constituents were for an ad hoc supergroup.

The central characters made a disparate triumvirate. John Baldry looked exotic in a fetching braided kaftan. Elton favoured a red bomber jacket over a 'Rocket Man' T-shirt, his outfit completed by gold platform boots. By comparison, Rod seemed almost demure in a floral patterned jacket and yellow trousers.

In years to come, Elton and Rod would become great mates and intermittent sparring partners. But it was Baldry's 'Top Of The Pops' promotion which had brought about their first substantive meeting of the 1970s.

Another cameo performance saw Elton, along with The Who's Keith Moon, become transient Beach Boys at a Crystal Palace concert.

These guest slots were quickly forgotten. *Honky Chateau* was a work to be remembered.

Taking its name from the place of conception – the Strawberry Studios in Chateau D'Herouville, thirty miles outside Paris – *Honky Chateau* succeeded in capturing on vinyl the exuberance of Elton's concert performance.

The first studio collection from his enlarged permanent band, *Honky Chateau* exhibited fresh impetus where *Madman Across The Water* had indicated creative stagnation.

A new and isolated environment had the desired restorative effect. 'For two weeks it was like the Motown hit family,' Elton enthused. 'Bernie was upstairs writing. Maxine was rushing down, correcting his spelling, throwing the lyrics on to the piano; then me working on them, with the band sitting around, waiting to play as soon as I'd finished.'

The result corresponded with the intent – a group LP high on simplicity and strong on melody.

Everything worked. Davey Johnstone slotted in as if a regular, jazz violinist, Jean-Luc Ponty, made a telling contribution, while permissible levity was injected by Legs Larry Smith, an erstwhile member of the anarchic Bonzo Dog Band – one of the notable respondents to the same Liberty Records' advertisement that Elton and Bernie individually answered.

Davey Johnstone remarked that a feature of the album was that there were no arrangements as such, just straight playing. From a personal standpoint, he was happy with his own contribution, 'as I hadn't played rock guitar before'.

Nigel Olsson expressed delight at the change in direction evidenced on the album. 'I'm glad the orchestral phase is over and we're into more of a band thing.'

While the lyrics and melodies were sacrosanct, he, Dee and Davey all contributed ideas to how the songs should be tackled: 'Elton has the most say, but it never comes to that. There's no "I'm the boss" thing.'

Dee Murray was appreciative of Elton's insistence that the quartet should be regarded as a group, as opposed to a star with three regular supporting musicians. 'At the beginning, we had it in our minds that we were backing him. But Elton made it quite clear that we weren't. To us it's obvious that he is the star. But with this band there is nothing wrong with that.'

Elton was saying less than had been previously standard. Relieved at the album's cordial reception, he had taken off for a rented mansion in Malibu to escape the physical and emotional pressures which had taken him to the point of collapse, necessitated the cancellation of an Italian tour and resulted in his placing under medical supervision.

Before this enforced summer break, Elton had become prone to morose moods, shouting at associates and exhibiting other signs of excessive stress.

'I was never worried from a musical point of view, but personality-wise I was unbearable,' he conceded. 'That was the pressure. I've had exhaustion bouts but never a nervous crack-up like that.'

From behind the drumkit, it was understandable for Nigel Olsson to dismiss fame as a phenomenon he had yet to properly consider because the band's commitments allowed no time for reflection. By the same token, the frenetic workload afforded scant opportunity to assimilate any suggestion of failure.

In the role of frontman, Elton could not share that oblivious luxury. If the songs got panned, they were his songs more than Bernie's. If concert reviews were negative, it was Elton the critics sniped at, rather than his three able lieutenants.

It had been necessary to bear the brunt of the vituperative response to *Madman Across The Water*, 'an album of immense pain, a very personal album'.

With retirement on his mind, it was fortunate that, in contrast, *Honky Chateau* had been a positive pleasure to compile. Elton attested that its recording had given him greater happiness than the sessions for the other LPs combined. 'And I love the Chateau,' he added. 'There's something about the place.'

The transition to a basic rock group format had also attracted a new phalanx of followers, as indicated by the chart progress of the second single from the LP, released as Elton braced himself for the next assault on America.

'Honky Cat', a joyous jazz-infected stomper, was a typical example of both the rapidity of Elton and Bernie's songwriting system and the band's facility for translating potential into product.

Said Davey Johnstone: 'Bernie brought down the song in the morning, Elton worked on it for about ten minutes, then the rest of us worked for a couple of hours on an arrangement. Two days later it was recorded.'

Back live in the States, Elton continued to set new standards. Playing before 19,000 people at the Philadelphia Spectrum, he broke a house record established by Elvis Presley. In Los Angeles, unabashed theatre matched inspired musicianship note for note.

Kissing a picture of Doris Day which had stood incongruously atop his piano, Elton thanked an ecstatic audience for 'the most fantastic night of my life'. The band were said to have been moved to tears by both performance and reception.

On his reappearance at Carnegie Hall, Legs Larry Smith wowed the punters in his own inimitable fashion.

The *New York Times* accurately recorded Legs Larry as making his concert entry 'dressed in a white suit with a long flowing veil and silver helmet topped with wedding cake decoration'.

It seemed almost incidental to add that the veil was borne by two midgets dressed as South American dictators.

For reasons not convincingly explained, the girl dance troupe, the Rockettes, had been recruited to join Elton and Legs Larry in a tap dancing extravaganza to 'Singing In The Rain.'

As a piece of showbiz bravado, it was certainly an upgrade on Elton performing 'I've Got A Lovely Bunch Of Coconuts' as a diversionary tactic when his amplifiers gave up the ghost in the early days. By future standards, it was nothing out of the ordinary.

The tour would have brought 1972 to a perfect conclusion, had Elton not been required to interrupt the American itinerary to dash to London for a forgettable performance at the Royal Variety Show.

With an unquestioned reputation for charity work, the artist's reluctance to participate in what is generally recognized as probably the most star-infested annual turkey cannot merely be attributed to standard pop-star cussedness.

'I thought I'd get bad publicity if I refused,' he confessed. 'What an awful show. As a musical event it was the biggest non-event of all time [and] the most horrendous two-day stretch I've ever had.'

At least the Royal Variety fiasco afforded Elton an opportunity to meet the artist he was compared to when reviewers could think of no one else . . . Liberace.

'Basically, he's a send up,' was the Elton evaluation. 'He knows it and flaunts it. I could not compete with him.'

On stage, maybe. But Elton's earnings had already taken him comfortably into the millionaire league and he was unafraid of ostentatious shopping.

From his earliest days in the money, Elton's generosity was legion. On the purchase of his first status symbol – a pale mauve Aston Martin – he gave away its predecessor.

As his earnings increased, so did the extravagance of his numerous kindnesses. Prestigious automobiles, a yacht, fine antiques and paintings by the masters were lavished on professional and personal nearest and dearest. But, as often the case, it was the less grandiose gestures which left the most lasting impression.

Newest to the band, Davey Johnstone had set his heart on a distinctive mandolin espied among the impressive inventory of New York music store, Manny's. Despite his acquisitive desire, Davey considered the 800 dollars price tag a little excessive for his budget. However, his frequent visits to the shop while agonizing over whether to purchase the instrument had not gone unnoticed.

Having made up his mind to buy the mandolin, Davey returned to Manny's to find that an anonymous customer had beaten him to the punch. Dispirited, the guitarist trudged back to the hotel, where he found the mandolin waiting for him. Elton had learned of Davey's dilemma and gone out and purchased it as a gift.

Naturally, charity began at home, and Elton had purchased 'Hercules', a rather fetching abode in the stockbrocker belt in Virginia Water, installing his mother and stepfather in a nearby residence.

In contrast, Bernie continued to favour life in the wilds of Lincolnshire, spending his home life in an unobtrusive cottage.

However, the lyricist was soon to join the Surrey set, becoming a near neighbour at Wentworth.

Bernie displayed no displeasure at his peripheral place in the fame game. It suited his character to live his life out of the limelight.

It was largely as a means of guaranteeing his writing partner a more equitable share of the huge earnings generated by their songs that Elton had added Bernie to his band. But lacking Elton's flair for the theatrical, his place in the chorus line was not always a fulfilling one.

His talent was the capacity to come up with a perfectly acceptable set of lyrics inside twenty minutes. Not bad for someone whose self-assessment was of 'a fairly lazy writer'.

Allied to Elton's facility for melody, the pairing could produce an album of material in a matter of days – or even sufficient songs for a double LP set, as *Goodbye Yellow Brick Road* was to prove.

They had carried on in their prolific way since 1967, the only hiatus being around *Madman Across The Water* – a period when Elton was under excessive strain and Bernie and Maxine had just got married.

Though favouring disparate lifestyles, a brotherly bond had developed between the two. As Bernie was to later remark: 'I call him ol' fat pig. He calls me little twerp. We're not serious.'

Similarly, for partners thrown together at the caprice of Ray Williams, they exhibited a remarkable consensus of taste when it came to their own writing.

Of songs from the early albums, 'Amoreena' (off *Tumbleweed Connection*) has remained close to the top of Elton's predilections. In parallel, Bernie described the lyrics as among those which instilled the greatest pride.

'It's a good song in the sense that it has a lot of natural feeling to it. It's a love song but it is a bawdy love song.'

Up to the autobiographical *Captain Fantastic* LP in 1975, Bernie contended that his songs never depicted personal experience. None the less, *Tumbleweed Connection* had been a showcase for the lyricist's fascination with things American – in particular, the Civil War.

'I love my western books and I'm just going to keep on building up a library.' He was also an avid collector of replica guns and other memorabilia – ' anything that bears any relevance that I can hang up.'

Exhibiting wry amusement at the myriad misinterpretations the American public had placed on some of his early lyrics, Bernie recalled phases when Stateside fans had steadfastly refused to accept that there was no ulterior meaning.

'They would come up with incredible things [like] racialism, anti-semitism, from "Border Song". Someone even said "I Need You To Turn To" was about the crucifixion.'

From *Honky Chateau* onwards, the lyrics could hardly have been more self-explanatory, the textbook example being the year's closing single.

'Crocodile Rock' was cogent pastiche from the rock music hall of fame. Elton described it as the nostalgia song he had yearned to compose. Listen closely, he advised, and spot the inspirational forces – the Beach Boys, Neil Sedaka. Eddie Cochran, et cetera.

If it had been made ten years later the song would have represented manna from heaven to an emergent video director. Yet so potent was the image elucidated that a promotional film would be superfluous. Eyes closed, an unrepentant Teddy Boy immediately bops into focus.

Meanwhile, Elton was playing Santa at his old school, visiting the junior section party at Pinner Grammar to present a colour television for the common room.

It was his second return to the school inside six months. The first was for a solo concert, an invitation from the sixth-form society being accepted with alacrity.

Though Elton was happy to play on the Pinner Grammar Steinway, he insisted on the transporting of his own amplification. After humping the star's equipment to and from the stages of massive auditoriums, Elton's roadies experienced an acute case of culture shock dragging the same apparatus into the premises of a north London school.

After three years of fantastic accomplishments, the revelations continued. Possibly the unlikeliest yet was Elton's British reincarnation as a teen idol.

In Newcastle, the local constabulary was called out to assist his safe passage from a live show. Fainting fans and teenybop screaming were other new elements in Elton's concert dates.

The reason? Probably that after the commercial nadir of *Madman Across The Water*, new home fans had been recruited by the greater accessibility of *Honky Chateau*, the jaunty single, 'Crocodile Rock', and its poignant successor, 'Daniel'.

As both 45s were advance tasters for the new album, *Don't Shoot Me I'm Only The Piano Player*, interest was at its apex when the LP was released in February 1973.

The album had been recorded the previous summer, after a period of relative quietude. The lessons digested from the scheduling mayhem which contributed to the failings of *Madman Across The Water*, sufficient time had been allotted for writing during the early part of 1972, a three-week college tour being the only major diversion.

Even so, when it came to the recording dates, Elton was in poor health. 'But I really wanted to do it and got it done in a couple of weeks. I can never bear farting about.'

Elton the film fan doubtless appreciated the publicity material for the new product. A loving parody of a movie poster, it transported the star into the era of Fred Astaire, with the band members getting supporting cast credits.

Elton the incipient accountant could hardly stifle satisfaction at the early returns.

Don't Shoot Me went straight in at number one in the BBC charts. In the same week, 'Crocodile Rock' topped the US singles listings while 'Daniel' stood at five in Britain.

Recorded at the same French studios as *Honky Chateau* and with Paul

Buckmaster back in less omnipresent harness, *Don't Shoot Me* was Elton at his eclectic best. Once through admiring the elegant packaging – incorporating a twelve-page booklet – purchasers could explore the artist's many musical facets. As well as the singles, there was 'Elderberry Wine', a straightforward rocker, the bluesy 'Have Mercy On The Criminal' and 'I'm Going To Be A Teenage Idol', a song dedicated to Marc Bolan.

In his capacity as an unequivocal T. Rex fan, Elton had recorded with the band, even becoming an honorary T. Rex member for one unforgettable 'Top Of The Pops' taping.

In the mode of 'Crocodile Rock', Elton partly considered the album a nostalgic work, affectionately focussing on the 1950s and 1960s. 'I use my voice a lot more, as I did on *Honky Chateau*, with a bit of double tracking. I sound like Bobby Vee or the Everly Brothers.'

For the artist, 'Daniel' – 'one of the "me" songs' – was a firm favourite. Not only did it sell prodigiously worldwide. It was a single on which Elton had staked his reputation before Dick James.

James was said to have counselled against the track's release in single form. Elton deemed it 'one of the best songs I've ever written' and insisted that it should be put out, irrespective of its hit potential. He even claimed to be paying for press advertising as DJM refused to defray the cost.

The truth lay somewhere in-between. Certainly, those in the label's hierarchy were unconvinced of the merits of the track as an A-side. Nor is there any dispute that Elton was adamant in wanting the single released and was prepared to meet the relevant costs. But Dick James sagely mediated to placate his star asset.

Whatever DJM's prior misgivings, 'Daniel' would be promoted with all the resources at the company's disposal. The theory was that if a hit ensued, all parties would benefit. If not, Elton would have no grounds for further complaint.

Elton considered that the change of style evidenced on *Honky Chateau* and *Don't Shoot Me* had been vindicated by the public reaction. While the former did considerably better business than *Madman*, the sales of the latter astounded him. The only debit had been the shedding of some earlier fans through either snobbery or genuine distaste at the more commercial fare.

'I had to prove that we could do something without a big orchestra,' Elton commented. 'Now we've expanded our audience, it's just a matter of trying to keep them there.'

Sandwiched between his British concerts and another mammoth American tour came a sporting first which induced a nervous condition way in excess of that occasioned by the odd local difference with his record label.

Accepting an invitation to play in a benefit match for Middlesex and England cricketer, Freddie Titmus, at the game's spiritual home of Lord's, Elton was awestruck as he walked on to the playing area via the sanctum of the pavilion. In comparison, dealing with his surprise elevation to the list of schoolgirl heart-throbs was plain sailing.

By the time Elton had jetted off to his forty-two city American tour, audiences on both sides of the Atlantic had been treated to a sneak preview of the next album – and first double LP set – *Goodbye Yellow Brick Road*.

'Saturday Night's Alright (For Fighting)' was a less than convincing example of rock with everything thrown in, the kitchen sink included, which only served to emphasize his strengths as a performer of emotive ballads and sixties-type pop.

Nevertheless, after *Don't Shoot Me*, nothing could diminish the interest in the double album, which was launched simultaneously in New York and Los Angeles in suitably lavish style.

Favoured press and television people gathered at both locations for a closed-circuit broadcast. John Reid and Gus Dudgeon directed the proceedings in LA; Bernie Taupin was in charge of the Big Apple première.

They could have stayed at home. Many artists have miscalculated in releasing a double LP. Elton himself acknowledged: 'Double albums are always dangerous because often the contents don't stand up.' With Elton on a roll, the tills kept on ringing.

Two more hits were to accrue, both obvious single material. The title track was the sort of transatlantic anthem that Elton and Bernie could write in their sleep. Ditto for 'Bennie And The Jets', a future American number one which was only released in Britain by DJM in 1976 after Elton had switched allegiance to his own Rocket label. The live feel of 'Bennie' is down to the ingenuity of Gus Dudgeon, who incorporated a tape of a past Festival Hall audience.

Similarly, MCA elected not to go with 'Candle In The Wind', Bernie's tribute to his idol, Marilyn Monroe, as an American A-side. DJM thought otherwise and were rewarded with another hit.

True to his nature of communicating all things to different journalists, Elton was quoted both as touting 'Candle In The Wind' for single release – ' I get goosebumps every time I play it' – and registered disappointment when Dick James Music complied, the putative grouse being that too much had already been taken off the album.

Although the song coincided with a resurgence of interest in the ill-fated screen godess, Bernie was at pains to stress that the lyrics were written out of admiration, not avarice.

Like Americana, Marilyn Monroe was an example of a Taupin interest making a rapid transition to obsession. Starting off with a few biographies, he had graduated to collectors' memorabilia – calendars, film stills and original posters, building into a major archive. True to the generous side of his nature, Elton had also sought out some Monroe rarities for his lyricist, including items of clothing.

Goodbye Yellow Brick Road brought Elton to a second career watershed. As one instance, it marked the end of a recording era, even though it was an album later than anticipated.

At the planning stage, the idea had been to record in Jamaica, as was becoming the vogue for headline acts. Gus Dudgeon was despatched as a one-man advance party to ascertain whether the studios could offer facilities comparable with the Chateau. Even a table football machine was promised.

Then, ensconced on the Caribbean, things appeared to be proceeding to plan. The material for the double LP was written in a matter of days while the band worked on their tans on the other side of the island. With twenty new songs and two outstanding from the *Don't Shoot Me* sessions, the sunbathing had to stop as the band rehearsed, in Elton's words, to the point where every track contender could be performed on stage as an old friend.

However, when it came to the actual recording, 'the mood and conditions weren't right,' a euphemism for a catalogue of disappointments. The piano didn't materialize, microphones failed to arrive and both band and producer were unhappy with the sound. So it was back to the favoured French studios for a farewell residency.

A change which was implemented for *Goodbye Yellow Brick Road* saw the engagement of Del Newman as arranger. In an 'all things to all men' utterance, Elton suggested that had he used Paul Buckmaster again, the press would have harangued him for using the same type of arrangement. Del had done a masterful job. But so had Paul on *Don't Shoot Me*, and he expected to work with them both again. How's that for consummate diplomacy?

In contrast, the divide between the star and DJM was hastening towards a chasm. It was with no great regret that Dick James passed over the full managerial reigns to John Reid in 1973. The publishing agreement with Dick James Music was also at an end, and both James and his son interpreted Elton's commitment to Rocket Records as a sure signal that he would not renew his recording contract when it expired in 1975.

Such circumstances were commonplace when an artist established himself in the supertax bracket. What genuinely upset the man to whom Elton often turned to for paternal advice on personal problems was how he would denigrate DJM in public, having said nothing (or the opposite) in private dealings.

A prime example was *Goodbye Yellow Brick Road*. In numerous interviews, the star squealed at the injustice of the double LP counting as only a single album for contract purposes – and the contract itself, stipulating two albums a year, as being deleterious to his creativity.

The DJM argument was that Elton only moaned retrospectively, and invariably to sources outside the company. As for the recording contract, Elton was no longer the naïve neophyte when it was renewed at the release of the seminal self-titled LP in 1970. He had been properly represented during the negotiations and well envisioned what would be entailed.

Dick James could hardly claim a vanguard role in the discovery of Elton John the recording artist. But he had backed others' judgements to the hilt out of the company budget. The thanks were to become further muted with the passage of time.

Illustrating that the 'Madman' still went over a storm across the water, the 1973 American tour proved another monster. The highlights were prestige gigs on the East and West Coast – respectively Madison Square Garden and the Hollywood Bowl, where the 40,000 tickets for his two shows were quickly snapped up. Nor were seats going begging at any of the other tour venues, which boasted capacities of between 15,000 and 25,000.

It was at the Bowl that Elton pulled out all the theatrical stops. The advance word of mouth was such that tickets had been reputedly changing hands for up to 500 dollars on the black market. Those unable to lay hands on one of the golden commodities had insult added to injury by a gigantic hoarding on Sunset Strip with a betoppered 'Elton' announcing a sell-out.

The real thing did not disappoint. A facsimile Elton in the top hat and tails motif, accompanied by a row of dancing girls, served as the backdrop. For company, a row of cardboard Eltons stretched out across the breadth of the stage.

The real Elton John made a grand entrance via a flight of glittering steps. As he did, five grand piano lids were elevated to spell out his name. As a flock of doves was released, the audience could have been forgiven for believing that they had been erroneously given tickets for a practice run for an Olympic Games' opening ceremony. Even sound man, Clive Franks, made an incognito appearance, being relieved of his duties for the dubious pleasure of donning a crocodile costume in support of the hit single.

Film director, Bryan Forbes, was in attendance to supervise coverage for an impending British television documentary, to additionally feature studio footage and interviews with Elton and Bernie.

His likely observation was that Tinsel Town's most talented sons would have been hard pressed to stage an equivalent spectacular. With the band in premium form, it was one of those special occasions.

By comparison, the Madison Square Garden show could almost be reviewed as reserved, although the white space cowboy apparel which had become the trademark of the tour was retained.

For the latest American excursion, Elton had hired an exotic creature comfort which alleviated some of the rigours of touring. As temporary owner of a luxurious Boeing aircraft, the Starship, he took full advantage of its living, recreational and resting facilities. There was even a Hammond organ on board.

However, for an exhausting tour, the plane's greatest benefit was in allowing his party to fly out to different gigs from the same hotel base. The only problem was that with a small entourage, the high-level home-from-home appeared deserted most of the time. 'The eight of us felt as if we were playing hide and seek,' Elton joked.

It was even utilized as a hired car, being once despatched to collect Stevie Wonder for a guest jamming appearance – his first after his serious injury in a car crash – joining the band on 'Honky Tonk Women', which had stayed the course as a rousing encore. On the journey to Boston, Wonder also provided some memorable in-flight entertainment.

Elton was still on air after returning from the States. His first Christmas single, 'Step Into Christmas', had been written and recorded in a day. A vaguely Spectoresque feel in Gus Dudgeon's production moved the artist to remark: 'I sound a bit like the Ronettes on it.'

Another indication of the burgeoning confidence of the John–Taupin writing team was that they were now writing songs specifically for other artists. An example was 'Let Me Be Your Car' for Rod Stewart's 1974 album, *Smiler*, which also found Elton on piano and in the chorus line.

But Elton was thinking one step ahead. With *Goodbye Yellow Brick Road* as the high point of his career to date, it was apposite to once again contemplate change, though in this case from a position of strength.

'It will have to be the turning point, because we've gone as far as we can with this type of sound.'

Meanwhile, an authentic new beginning had seen Elton preside at the birth of his own label. The portents for Rocket Records as a showcase for original talent were hardly encouraging.

Apple, launched with egalitarian zeal by the post–*Pepper* Beatles, had withered to a bankrupt core having, at best, afforded transient fame to a handful of acts. Then there were the Rolling Stones' eponymous label and the Moody Blues' Threshold, serving as little more than outlets for the records of their famous figureheads.

That was not the way Elton or the street-smart John Reid envisaged Rocket, which signed up its first artists in 1973–4. And what a catholic bunch they were.

Kiki Dee – or rather Bradford-born Pauline Matthews – had then much in common with contemporary, Elkie Brooks. Great voice, good looks and a conspicuous lack of commercial achievement.

Common denominators with Elton included age and a past record deal with Philips. In Kiki's case her Philips' releases in the mid 1960s garnered considerable attention as she performed in the vein popularized by the emergent star roster of the black Detroit-based label, Tamla Motown.

Therefore, her subsequent signing to Tamla promised belated fame and fortune. She cut an album, *Great Expectations*, which palpably failed to fulfil its title, and her career was making little headway at the time of signing. With hindsight, the most fortuitous aspect of her Tamla tenure was crossing paths with John Reid.

Stackridge were a group of West Country funsters, who'd given the world such unforgettable ditties as 'Dora The Female Explorer'. An exemplary opening act – as they were to confirm at Elton's Wembley Stadium gig in 1975 – but with limited sales potential.

Difficult, too, to see how Longdancer would set the cash registers ringing. A folk rock combo, their biggest claim to fame was the inclusion of Nigel Olsson's brother.

In America, the label recruited Neil Sedaka, a remnant of pre-Beatles innocence. 'Calendar Girl', 'Oh Carol' and 'Breaking Up Is Hard To Do' were classics of their period before the one-time concert pianist bowed to the less innocent mood of the 1960s and concentrated on writing for others.

Lured back into recording by RCA in the early 1970s, he found a new audience for his material.

Others latterly more famous were rumoured to have slipped through Rocket's net as their asking price could not be met. Those said to have been turned down included Queen, Cockney Rebel, Ace and even the Beatle who didn't play guitar or write many songs. The mistakes at Apple would not be repeated. Can't pay, won't pay.

Nevertheless, Elton's intention was to properly remunerate those who had been signed.

'I'm appalled by the lack of knowledge of some people who have a lot of power in the music business,' he declared. 'It really frustrates me. As a reaction against it Rocket will offer a decent deal with a good royalty rate.'

He added that he intended Rocket to be known as a friendly company. The onus would be on its signings, rather than him, as he was still contracted to DJM.

'Ideally, we're trying to open a record company that's for the artist, both creatively and money-wise. I want to be completely open to any type of music.

'I'm into a lot of black music and if I ever met a good reggae act I'd love to do that too. On the other hand, it'd be nice to find a nice young group with the energy of Slade.'

Bernie was also involved in the label's talent search. His preference was for a young aggressive band with originality and good stage appearance.

'We'd like anyone with material to get in touch with us. I'm sure they'll all get a reply.'

Aside from Elton and Bernie, John Reid, Gus Dudgeon and Steve Brown were involved in the administration of the enterprise in the first year.

As *Madman Across The Water* had completed the first cycle in the development of the Elton John Band, *Goodbye Yellow Brick Road* was the culmination of the second stage.

With fond memories, it was *au revoir* Chateau D'Herouville and hello to the picturesque setting of the rocky mountains of Denver, Colorado and the Caribou ranch, where a studio at 9,000 feet fully tested altitude acclimatization.

Why Denver? 'It was time for a change. Even if we hadn't gone to Caribou, we would still have changed studio.'

The Caribou period was one of extensive readjustment for Elton. He was looking to further augment the line-up, possibly through the introduction of a keyboards player to allow him more scope in live performance.

Percussionist, Ray Cooper, had achieved permanency in the band during the preceding British tour, by making 'an incredible difference to the sound and visual aspect of the group'.

A respected session musician who had spent a year in the band, Blue Mink, Ray would have been an invaluable recruit for his stage antics alone. As put succinctly by one of Elton's aides: 'A maniac during live performances but as quiet as a vicar after the shows.'

Off-stage, the signs were that Elton's involvement as a football club executive would require a greater provision of time. Elsewhere, the formative days of Rocket were proving that awareness of the mistakes of other superstar label bosses was no guarantee against similarly costly misjudgements.

Yet, at the year's inception, the five Rocket heads had exuded quiet confidence.

'Amoureuse' was not merely an ambitious top twenty entry. It had pushed Kiki Dee into prominence after a decade as a nearly girl and suggested that Rocket had unearthed a major talent of potential longevity in its first batch of signings.

'Before Rocket, I'd been in the business for nine years,' Kiki explained. 'I'd changed everything from name to hair colouring without it making any difference. I was very disheartened.'

It was a case of business acumen capitalizing on fortune when, with her professional life in the doldrums, Kiki had rung up John Reid to request the telephone number of a mutual friend.

'John asked me what I was doing. When I told him "nothing", he replied, "we want you". I think that at one stage, Elton and John Reid had wanted to sign Dusty Springfield, but nothing came of it.'

Kiki's vocal ability had never been in doubt. But encouraged by Elton, she contributed four songs to her long-playing Rocket début, *Loving And Free*.

Elton and Bernie had also been among the songwriters, furthering their exploration into the previously uncharted territory of composing with artists other than Elton in mind.

'We've always refused when people have asked us to write for them because we didn't think it would work,' Elton said in 1973. 'We decided to write for Kiki because we were desperate to change her image from the sort of "bouffant singer from the Latino in South Shields" to what she really is.

'Bernie's recovering from having to write Kiki's songs from a girl's angle!'

Elton had professed himself happier with Kiki's breakthrough than any of his own personal accomplishments in 1973 – American tour and number one records included.

The problem was that for every hit, there were a handful of hard luck stories – and a horror tale reminiscent of Apple. For example, Rocket signed up a thirteen-year-old Welsh boy, Maldwyn Pope Thomas, to a lengthy contract.

Admittedly, the lad came on the highest recommendation – John Peel, who had passed on a tape submitted to him. When Maldwyn's voice broke, the bank didn't, but it was indicative of the mounting mayhem at the label.

The recording, the touring, the label, the gladhanding. Something had to give. It was Elton.

Commitments dictated that the *Caribou* LP was completed in ten days to allow for tour dates in Japan, Australia and New Zealand. Meanwhile, the wheels were being put in motion for a seventeen-date British tour in the spring, intended to commence in the picturesque setting of Paignton, working its way to a grand metropolis finale at the Empire Pool, Wembley, a month later.

That, however, was before an unsavoury incident in New Zealand highlighted Elton's need for a break from the cumulative pressures.

From a performance viewpoint, the New Zealand trip could be adjudged a success, with a 35,000 crowd breaking the attendance record for a single show.

Off-stage, it was a spot of illegal hit-making which attracted the police, judiciary and headlines.

The incident occurred at a press reception in Auckland and, according to Elton, stemmed from the alleged mismanagement of the event.

In his version of events, an argument developed over a shortage of refreshments, both liquid and solid. Consequently, the organizers were treated to a burst of the temper feared by John Reid's employees when their work did not meet his satisfaction. On this occasion, though, Reid's ire extended beyond invective. In the ensuing fracas a woman writer was hurt and the trouble continued at a nightspot.

Elton claimed that members of his entourage were being threatened and that the source of the threats was a local journalist.

'I went up, seized him by the collar and was just about to clock him round the face when my manager stepped in and hit him for me.'

Although Elton felt aggrieved at his and Reid's subsequent treatment by police and magistrates, he was discharged without conviction. Reid was given a brief custodial sentence.

The enforced lull in activity caused by this brush with the law did have one advantage, Elton conceded. 'When all the trouble started and my manager was sent to prison, we had time to talk. We all decided we were physically exhausted and the thought of going on another tour for the time being was impossible.'

Thus, a fortnight after the British tour dates had been announced in the music press, the same papers carried a statement that the dates would be cancelled owing to the 'severe strain' Elton and the group had been under during recent months.

Elton would now honour only two of his original live commitments – a performance at Watford FC and a fund-raiser for invalid children at the Royal Festival Hall.

The latter, performed in the presence of Princess Margaret, formed the basis for one side of the deservedly maligned live LP, *Here And There*, the last album for DJM, aside from compilations.

The concert itself raised in excess of £10,000, for which the royal party had an opportunity to thank the band when they dined together after the show. Princess Margaret was a genuine Elton fan, and two of the star's proudest possessions were a pair of stuffed leopards she had given to him.

In terms of venue and audience, Elton at Watford seemed light years away. Donning his football historian's hat, the star could not remember a bigger crowd at Vicarage Road than the 40,000 who came to see him, openers, Nazareth and guest star, Rod Stewart, a one-time apprentice player at Brentford.

Appropriately garbed in the Watford colours of yellow and black, Elton's set included the Beatles' 'Lucy In The Sky' – a surprising selection to a world unaware that before the year's end, a studio version of the song would be available. This heralded the arrival of Rod Stewart, amid widespread waving of tartan scarves.

Backed by Elton's band, Rod performed 'Country Comfort', 'Sweet Little Rock 'N' Roller' and 'Angel', leaving Elton to close the show with 'Saturday Night's Alright.'

It was a magical day for the star in every sense. On home territory, he could do no wrong, even down to leading the audience in 'Singing In The Rain' when the elements misbehaved.

The pointers were that Elton intended to exceed the peripheral function of Watford's star follower. At the press launch for the concert, he proudly sported the team kit, before proceeding to exhibit his goalkeeping prowess for the benefit of photographers. Attendant scribes were left to feign enthralment as he exclusively revealed the club's average rise in home crowds over the season.

Then, for his twenty-seventh birthday, he chose to celebrate at a party for footballer, Ian Morgan.

June produced the *Caribou* LP, which sounded as it was conceived – in conditions of haste and harassment. Problems in the studio outside the band's control necessitated the tracks being cut in three to four days. Close to breaking point, Elton then considered himself unhappy with the vocals.

An instance of emotion commensurate with the studio altitude saw an enraged singer threatening Gus Dudgeon with all manner of unpleasantries should he dare include 'Don't Let The Sun Go Down On Me' on the LP.

At one stage, the song's backing vocals included a smattering of Beach Boys, Dusty Springfield, Danny Hutton (Three Dog Night) and

America. 'If that session had worked out, it would have been incredible. Unfortunately, it all got a bit chaotic.'

Eventually, with the supporting cast trimmed down to just Beach Boys, Bruce Johnston and Carl Wilson, it was the stand out track.

Not that there was excessive competition. 'The Bitch Is Back' – a not quite convincing rocker in the mode of 'Saturday Night's Alright' – provided a contrast in the chosen singles, which did particularly well in the States. Of the rest, the most charitable that can be said was that the ideas merited better execution.

Elton had prompted Bernie into writing 'Grimsby', 'because Randy Newman had written a song about Cleveland and I thought we could make it sound like the Beach Boys.' The star had additionally been the motivating force behind 'Solar Prestige A Gammon', 'which is total lunacy. I actually feel quite guilty about that.'

Defence being the best form of attack, the star claimed that the lukewarm critical reception had been anticipated: 'I thought *Caribou* would get slagged off because it was time for something of mine to get slagged. I'm just sitting back and taking it.'

More candidly, Elton subsequently proclaimed of the LP: 'It's a miracle it came out because of all the pressure within the group, especially with me. I'd just about had it with everything. I was cracking up.' With fatigue causing, then aggravating personality problems, the best things to result from the first wave of Caribou recording were not included on the eponymous platter.

Nigel Olsson exhibited an exemplary vocal talent on a cover of the Bee Gees' 'Only One Woman'. For Elton himself, the thrill of recording 'Lucy In The Sky' was accentuated by John Lennon's participation in the session.

Having established a rapport with the former Beatle during a meeting in Los Angeles the previous year, Lennon then played him some rough mixes of tracks for the *Walls And Bridges* LP in New York. Elton didn't need asking twice to contribute to the album – even though at the outset, his involvement was to be confined to 'oohs and aahs'.

'I've never met anybody so inspiring,' recounted an awestruck Elton. 'You just instantly fall in love with him when you meet him. I was just knocked out that he would even go into a studio with me . . . I'm that much of a fan.'

From 'oohs and aahs', Elton's involvement on the Lennon LP was upgraded within hours to piano and vocals on two tracks – 'Whatever Gets You Thru The Night' and 'Surprise Surprise'.

Invited to reciprocate, Lennon arrived at Caribou to play guitar on 'Lucy In The Sky'. 'He had a good time, except he couldn't get used to the altitude,' Elton joked. 'He had to keep rushing to the oxygen tank.'

Reasoning that if he was going to record one Lennon song, he might just as well do two, Elton also recorded the *Mind Games*' track, 'One Day At A Time', 'one of my favourite numbers'.

Another link with the Beatles was 'Snookeroo', a song tailored by Elton and Bernie to Ringo Starr's background, personality and vocal range. Included on Ringo's LP, *Goodnight Vienna*, it was a top three record in America.

Playing on the sessions for the album, Elton found himself in the company of musicians of the calibre of The Band's Robbie Robertson. The incontrovertible fact that his records had conspicuously outsold theirs failed to alleviate his feeling of inferiority going into the studios. It was Reg Dwight in the company of those he had idolized when working behind a record shop counter.

'I thought "whoops I've got to play well here", then realized I could play just as well as they could . . . What a silly sod!'

A holiday on a tennis ranch in Arizona was one method of relaxation for Elton after the myriad frustrations of the album sessions and the New Zealand fracas. It also marked a departure from the normal pattern of leisure activities, being his first solo vacation for four years.

Returning refreshed, he commented that in contrast to the despairing outlook of February, he now genuinely couldn't wait to get back on the road – especially when the immediate prospect was to perform before his adoring American followers.

Though his attitudes were to alter, at this juncture, Elton could not countenance touring as an obligation grudgingly fulfilled.

'The whole reason to tour is to strive for something better. Forget about the costumes and staging – it's the music that counts. If you don't keep improving, you're wasting your time.'

Thus from late September it was near enough business as usual as Elton commenced a 43–date tour in Dallas.

For one still relatively unaccustomed to luxuriant life on the road, touring partner, Kiki Dee, was having fun making the transition to exclusive travelling arrangements.

'To me, it was exciting to be doing my first American gigs in such amazing company, helped by Elton's love and a police escort to a private plane. Elton had a suite at the back and there was what we referred to as the hippy room, with cushions that people lounged around on and socialized.'

Prestige-wise, the jewel in the crown was a four-night stint at the 18,000 Los Angeles Forum. Initially, the schedule allowed for three concerts, but as all tickets were snatched up within six hours of the box office opening, a fourth was agreed. Another additional show in Washington was prompted by a near riot of unlucky applicants.

In moments of self-doubt, the artist himself would ring up the venues to check that all tickets had actually been sold: 'It's hard to believe sometimes.'

Proving that Elton was the star other luminaries left their heavily guarded abodes to see, the guest list for the Forum shows comprised an eclectic variety bill – Rod Steiger, Harry Nilsson, Ringo Starr, David Cassidy, Steve McQueen, Barbra Streisand, Diana Ross and Liz Taylor.

With greater opportunities to play tennis and no shortage of offers for disc-jockeying stints at local radio stations, Los Angeles seemed a preferable alternative to the English stockbroker belt. Rife speculation about Elton's future living arrangements was further fuelled by rumours that he had purchased a local residence.

In the eyes of the American public, Elton was a studio prince and a concert king. Whereas England treated him, he felt, with cold indifference, he was an unquestioned hot property across the Atlantic.

A less punitive taxation system can only have enhanced America's suitability as a permanent base, a factor doubtless stressed by his financial advisers.

Many other British rock stars (McCartney excepted) had arranged periods of foreign residency as a tax shelter. Rumours abounded that Elton would announce plans to move to the US in 1975.

But he arrived back in Britain before Christmas to dispel speculation with a declaration of loyalty. 'I thought seriously about staying in the States but had to accept the reality – that I simply couldn't face it. Anyway I've now made enough money to live happily in Britain … whatever the taxman may take from me.'

The British taxman was to have good cause to appreciate Elton's patriotism during the twelve months ahead.

Buoyed by the US tour, rated by many observers as his finest to date, he looked back with affection and forward with confidence. His only concert mishap had been characteristically bizarre. A smoking pipe thrown from the audience in Greensboro, North Carolina, scored an accidental bullseye.

Once the band was convinced that Elton's collapse was no prank, he was carried off stage. More shocked than hurt he sheepishly returned after a few minutes' respite.

In contrast, the highspot – if not the most accomplished perform- ance – had been the New York Thanksgiving Day concert at Madison Square Garden, where Elton made public knowledge of a barely kept secret by announcing: 'As it's Thanksgiving, we thought we'd give you a special present. So here's something to be thankful for. . . .' Right on cue, John Lennon entered to a tumultuous ovation, the equal of any received during the Beatles' touring days.

The live liaison extended to three numbers – 'Lucy In The Sky', 'Whatever Gets You Thru The Night' and 'I Saw Her Standing There' – the latter giving Lennon particular gratification as the song was McCartney territory.

If Elton's boundless admiration for Lennon made him tense about the impending performance, the thought of facing an audience engendered equal unease in his fêted playing partner.

Recalled Kiki Dee: 'Lennon was so nervous, he asked Davey Johnstone to string his guitar for him, which I thought was quite sweet.'

Covering the MSG concert – and the formal bash that ensued at the straight-laced Hotel Pierre – society magazine, the *New Yorker*, amplified Elton's thoughts by dwelling on Lennon elbowing his way through the throng in an attempt to gain an audience with the host.

'Our idea of reality would be Elton John trying to elbow his way through the crowd to get to John Lennon's table.' Nevertheless, one can only assume that the ex-Beatle elicited some ironic pleasure from the incident.

The same applied to the acclaim accorded Elton's recorded version of 'Lucy In The Sky', recognized as one of the most convincing cover versions of a Lennon and McCartney song.

At the outset, Elton had only intended it as an addition to his concert repertoire of other artists' classics. It was the audience reaction it generated which persuaded him to attempt a studio version.

Bernie Taupin deserves maximum credit as the source of the initial idea to perform the track live. Elton's preference had been for the Stylistics' 'Rockin' Roll Baby'.

Following what amounted to a declaration of allegiance to the Crown it was fitting that Elton's year should end on a high note in Britain.

In 1973, he had entered the Christmas show market with what he claimed veered perilously close to a pantomine. The trouble had emanated from the polystyrene snow.

'I couldn't play and I couldn't sing. The snow was too thick. It just wedged all the piano keys together and we ground to a halt.' Fingers crossed against repetition, the Hammersmith Odeon was hired for five Christmas specials.

This time, no disasters befell the festive gigs, showcasing a superlative three-hour performance. It was merely a catastrophe not to be in attendance. An immaculate blending of rock and theatre, the tone was perfectly established by a frighteningly lifelike Elton dummy whizzing down from the circle to the stage.

BBC Television viewers gleaned only a fraction of the electric atmosphere from the segment broadcast live as Elton and the band – augmented by the Muscle Shoals Horns – ran the gamut from 'Skyline Pigeon' to 'White Christmas', this time to the accompaniment of a benign deluge of polystyrene snow.

Putting it into perspective, one reviewer opined: 'The Pope should never have tried to follow an act like that.'

Christmas was a less festive time at Rocket, where the optimism of the previous year had been replaced by concern at aspects of the company's administration.

The impetus the label had gained by the charting of 'Amoureuse' had tailed off in the succeeding months as the manifold drawbacks to co-operative management started to dawn on the founding fathers. Simultaneously, the early altruism began to evaporate.

While Elton derided the popular misconception that his own money had launched the label – the truth, he said, was that an advance had been supplied by MCA – there was no mistaking his distress at how the cash had been utilized.

Crisis gatherings proliferated, Steve Brown left of his own volition and there were staff and expenditure cuts.

With parental pride, Elton recounted the tale of how all on the Rocket payroll – secretaries and tea boy included – had taken a day trip to watch Kiki in concert. Yet the family was slowly disintegrating.

Longdancer weren't around for long after recording the label's respective first single and LP. The band's true curio value in rock history was later assured when Dave Stewart progressed, via The Tourists, to form the Eurythmics with Annie Lennox.

Kiki Dee remembered Stewart as 'a character even then as the young hippy, with long hair and cuban-heel boots.'

Other artists being only fleetingly accommodated, it was left to Kiki to provide the light at the end of the tunnel with a first American and second British hit, 'I've Got The Music In Me'.

While still believing in Rocket as 'a young and forward looking company,' she could also foresee the pitfalls. 'It is often the case that in labels run by artists, the artists are slightly naïve. It is not enough to be idealistic.'

Compensation for the lukewarm welcome accorded *Caribou* were the phenomenal sales of the first greatest hits compilation, which topped the British and American album charts going into 1975. With 'Lucy In The Sky' also heading the US singles listings, an expectant record-buying public awaited the summer release of *Captain Fantastic And The Brown Dirt Cowboy*, an autobiographical work previewed by Elton as 'more or less our experiences up to *Empty Sky* in song form.'

Not that Elton was ever out of the news for long. Readers of American newspaper, the *National Star*, voted him 'King of Rock'. With 'Lucy In The Sky', he had made history as the first non-Beatle to take a Beatles' song to number one in the Billboard listings. But he must have been heartily sick of the number when guesting on a Cher television special for CBS. Reportedly, it was on the eighth take that 'Lucy' was finally performed to his satisfaction.

A new Kevin Ayers LP featured him guesting on keyboards. A Kiki Dee concert at the Fairfield Hall, Croydon, found him contentedly clapping on stage, while supplying backing vocals.

In furtherance of his football commitments, he was even prepared to star in the bracket of venue he had continually sworn to forsake. To aid the benefit of a stalwart Watford player, Elton gave a concert at local nightspot, Baileys, that will live in the memory of all present. Extratime for the house band was rendered unnecessary as – in a precursor of future preference – Elton opted to do the entire performance solo.

Palpably nervous, he confided to the audience: 'I'm terrified doing this job on my own. You're in a good singing mood tonight, aren't you?'

Evidence of his anxiety was a bout of temporary amnesia on, of all numbers, 'Your Song'. But having humourously extricated himself, he went on to give a triumphant performance in this most incongruous of settings.

Another triumph of sorts was his celluloid début. The impending release of *Tommy* had him reminiscing over his short time on the film set and fulsome in his praise of its outrageous director, Ken Russell.

Elton – whose involvement in the movie had been completed in three days – acknowledged that his performance could barely be construed as acting, more like miming to a backing track on 'Top Of The Pops'. Apposite that, as British television's longest running chart show was avowedly not in his good books.

He had refused to appear on 'Top Of The Pops' in protest at a Musicians' Union ruling allowing artists only three hours of studio time – at their own expense – to pre-record a song scheduled for inclusion in the programme. What particularly irked Elton was that only the 'Top Of The Pops' orchestra could add the string parts.

Encapsulated in a statement: 'The Elton John Band and their producer, Gus Dudgeon, are in the habit of spending a great deal of time and love on perfecting each number they record. It is completely impossible to reproduce such labour at short notice'

The single responsible for the furore was one of considerable merit. 'Philadelphia Freedom' was inspired by the local entry in the now defunct World Team Tennis league, led by one of Elton's sporting pals, Billie Jean King. Maintaining the American theme in the year before the bicentennial, the arrangements were by Gene Page, the man who had inserted melody into the muttered love paeans of Barry White. This successful adaptation of the Philly sound was an early pointer towards Elton's future involvement with the legendary Philly producer, Thom Bell.

A powerful slab of orchestrated pop, its B–side afforded an opportunity to thank John Lennon for 'Lucy In The Sky' through the live version of 'I Saw Her Standing There', recorded at Madison Square Garden and featuring the ex-Beatle.

Thus both sides of the single – another number one for Elton in the USA – had especial relevance to the performer.

Drawn on to the topic of sport by an American magazine, he had confessed: 'If I could really go back and do anything, I'd like to be the singles champion at Wimbledon.'

His form in opening 'friendly' games with ultra-competitive Billie Jean suggested the aspiration to be wishful thinking. However, the two struck up a firm friendship, another product of which was the tennis star's elevation to backing vocalist.

Billie Jean remembers Elton's enthusiastic support for the Philadelphia team in the tennis league. 'When he was in town, he'd come to the matches and holler and have a good time.'

The top name in tennis fashion, Teddy Tinling, was commissioned to make a Philadelphia Freedoms warm-up suit for the team's famous fan.

Never one to be outdone in the generosity stakes, Elton promised to write a song for Billie Jean. There was an additional motive for the gesture.

Perceptibly improving on the tennis court, Elton attributed much of the credit to the bespectacled Wimbledon multi-champion. 'It's great being able to play with someone of that standard,' he enthused, elaborating that three minutes on court with Billie Jean imbued skills which had lain dormant in matches against 'play for fun' opposition.

He had also encountered another American tennis great, Jimmy Connors, in doubles partnership with Billie Jean – 'I wouldn't be stupid enough to play him on my own.'

When Elton had himself partnered Connors, Jimbo suddenly found the sport more enjoyable than it ever appeared on Centre Court. His appreciation of Elton's game extended to dissolving into a laughing heap on every occasion the singer managed a decent shot.

Off-court, Elton confided his wariness of sliding back, by default, into the cabaret circuit he had so gratefully left behind with Bluesology.

Yet from the sidelines, John Reid was confidently predicting: 'Every star's career has it's ups and downs. But Elton has been too big, has built up too great a following, to lose it all.' With these thoughts on board, it was time to take a few risks.

An approach by promoter, Mel Bush, for Elton to headline a Wembley Stadium concert in June, promised the star his biggest ever UK live audience. It also gave him the impetus for the first of a series of agonizing career decisions.

After nearly six years working with Dee Murray and Nigel Olsson, Elton felt it was time to change his band. The caring soul in him spent two months working up the courage to inform the affected parties. The coward took over to impart the news by telephone before the astute communicator softened up the media reaction by granting a series of interviews dwelling on the new at the expense of the immediate past.

In his defence, a high profile concert would not generally be considered as the ideal inauguration for an untried line-up.

At the time, Elton could offer no major attributable cause for the sackings. 'It wasn't a personality clash or anything like that. It was just something I felt inside,' he opined. 'I'd never fired anyone in my life before. . . It was awful.'

If parting was sorrowful for Elton, how should Dee and Nigel feel? Utterly loyal for five years, they had been expected to endure the same punitive round of recording and live dates.

Fresh – if that isn't a misnomer – from what were acknowledged as Elton's best concerts and the sessions on what was to become another monster selling album, the cursory dismissal notices must have rankled.

Elton offered disparate statements of mitigation. The suggestion that the founder members might take umbrage at the inclusion of new musicians didn't stand close scrutiny, Ray Cooper and Davey Johnstone having both been quite happily integrated over the years.

If Dee had been genuinely unhappy at the volume of concerts, as Elton had also claimed, it would have been easy for him to depart of his own volition. As for references to Nigel having a solo career, Davey Johnstone had managed one quite happily within the confines of the band. And Phil Collins's boost to the status of singing drummers was an innovation of the future.

Nigel certainly displayed no inkling of what was in store when he predicted at the turn of the year: 'I can't see myself leaving Elton because we're too close. The band is like a family.'

Now the group member with the longest tenure, Davey's role in the night of the apologetic long knives was spotlighted by Elton's disingenuous aside that he had been apprised of, and approved, the changes.

A more accurate interpretation of his guitarist's feelings was explained by Kiki Dee, his girlfriend of the time. 'Having been kept on, Davey was in an awkward position. Obviously, he felt sorry for Dee and Nigel, yet didn't want to antagonize Elton. I didn't know, and still don't, the ins and outs of the situation, beyond the knowledge that Elton genuinely wanted a change. What was questionable was the way it was done.'

According to Elton, his erstwhile drummer was the more forgiving of the departees. While deeply hurt, Nigel's feelings had been partly assuaged by a dinner invite and the promise of a song towards his solo career, which would now proceed with enforced emphasis.

Signed to Rocket and having John Reid as manager, pragmatism was Nigel's best option.

With Dee, the summarily dismissal continued to wound. The

invitation to dinner fell on stony ground and there was no individual project to proffer a song towards. In classic understatement, Elton said of Dee: 'He's a little hurt and I can understand that.'

Elton considered that Davey Johnstone now possessed all the necessary qualifications to be considered the unofficial leader of the enlarged group.

The Elton John Band Mark II also retained the manic percussionist, Ray Cooper, a fixture for the past eighteen months, to whom the star paid tribute: 'He takes a lot of work off me as far as the visuals go. I can have a rest every now and again because I know he's having a bit of a leap about.'

In to augment Ray and Davey were drafted two respected Americans – Kenny Passarelli (bass), formerly with Joe Walsh, and session keyboardsman, James Newton Howard, whose recruitment was the product of a job interview bizarre even for the rock business.

Invited to meet the star, Newton Howard was played the impending LP, offered – and accepted – employment, and then told he had a plane to catch. He may have wondered what he was letting himself in for. But he still made the flight.

Elton had decided that the level of orchestration on the *Fantastic* album made imperative the inclusion of another keyboard player for live performances. Of Newton Howard, he said: 'I need him to do Moog and other things like that. I can't just fiddle around with knobs. I want to stick to playing the piano and singing.'

Significantly, he had professed displeasure at the quality of his vocals during the last American tour – 'bloody abysmal' was the most stringent self-analysis.

To replace Nigel Olsson, Elton's choice was Roger Pope, formerly with Kiki Dee's band. Completing the changed combination, Elton recruited Caleb Quaye, without whom he might still be a session musician writing songs for others. Both Quaye and Pope had featured on some of Elton's earliest recordings, before reuniting in Hookfoot, one of DJM's less profitable signings. Acknowledging past debts, Elton had been effusive in praise of Hookfoot in advertisements for their records, additionally using the band as a support act.

When the dust had settled over the mode of hirings and firings, a relieved Elton announced to the press that it would be a long time before he contemplated a similar upheaval.

'I think this band will be better eventually because it's more powerful and there's more scope musically,' he declared, reasoning that with an increased personnel, the rock 'n' roll numbers would come across as subtle, rather than frantic, in live performance. Nevertheless, he publicly confessed to being nervous about the Wembley gig.

'I know people have said this band doesn't sound as good as the old band, but it's going to take time.'

The new line-up rehearsed for ten hours daily in a film studio outside of Amsterdam, playing one invitation only set for the Dutch press and selected fans.

Everything should have been geared up for the stadium concert. However, events on the day justified Elton's apprehension.

Basking in glorious thoughts of his percentage from a full house, the promoter could engage in magnanimous appreciation of the star's appeal across the spectrum: 'We've had heads, hippies, film stars, lords and ladies here today.'

Yet coming on at the end of a long and fulfilling bill, the new Elton John band not only had to compete with the memories of the Eagles and Joe Walsh. The Beach Boys had just exited to a rapturous ovation after a blissful translation of California sounds to a receptive north London.

For once in his performing life, Elton had been upstaged. There was nothing culpable in the musicianship. Nor could Clive Franks be faulted on the sound.

It was just that after a long day, a tired and often emotional audience wanted to be entertained with the songs they knew and loved. If some of the Wembley interpretations of Elton standards lacked their erstwhile dazzle, the prospect of the unexpurgated version of *Captain Fantastic* led many to vote with their feet.

Obviously, the LP had great personal significance for Elton, being an autobiographical account of the John–Taupin partnership's early adventures down the dark cul-de-sacs of Tin Pan Alley. Notwithstanding, there is a time and place for performing unfamiliar material in a one-hour slab – and it is certainly not before a 72,000 stadium audience, not all of whom are fans.

As with all miscalculations, Elton will have noted the muted reaction.

In retrospect, the LP is deserving of more respect than it received on release. Maybe reviewers considered the lavish packaging was designed to camouflage a tepid product. Perhaps the reaction was a natural one in view of the advance hype. Doubts were even expressed at Dick James Music, where Elton was asked to meet the cost of the album sleeve, depicting a fantasy sequence illustrated by Alan Aldridge. The insider's view was that the cover – 'over-expensive and over-indulgent' – reflected the thinking within the company about the vinyl content.

For the diehard fan, there was certainly much to assimilate before committing the stylus to action. One of two generously illustrated accompanying booklets contained the lyrics. The other took the reader through the maze of early trials and tribulations of the Captain (Elton) and the Cowboy (Bernie) by way of a varyingly accurate plethora of press cuttings.

An additional feature was a four-page 'not totally factual' cartoon strip taking a pre-school Reg to a post-discovery Elton.

While hardly his definitive work, the LP scores as a wistful adieu to the first phase of his creativity. Unarguably self-obsessed, it remains infinitely preferable to its patchy contemporaries – *Caribou* and *Rock Of The Westies*, the last studio album for DJM.

'Tell Me When The Whistle Blows' recalled the difficulty experienced by young country boy, Bernie Taupin, in making the transition to big city life when he first joined Elton in London. As implied by the title, he took the train to Lincolnshire at every opportunity.

'Better Off Dead' took a more bizarre theme, being inspired by examples of life's flotsam and jetsam as witnessed by the duo when they repaired to a West End hamburger bar in the wee small hours after some of their earliest sessions at Dick James' studio. 'Half the people who came in looked as if they'd be better off dead. The song's really about that.'

More straightforwardly, '(Gotta Get A) Meal Ticket' articulated the dilemma of Elton and Bernie in the early songwriting days at Dick James Music, while 'Bitter Fingers' found the duo sick of the 'tra la las' and 'la de das' required for Eurovision glory or prospective Cilla Black recordings.

'Someone Saved My Life Tonight', chronicled his suicidal state of mind after the unhappy end to his first serious heterosexual relationship.

In later years, Elton was able to laugh off 'suicide' attempts as an immature reaction. . . . 'Very "look I'm falling apart. I need more attention." There are times when you feel "I can't cope anymore". But you have to.'

Ironically, it was in America in 1975, at the peak of his fame, when he went up to his hotel room and took eighty-five tablets. Elton's embellished version of events had him immediately rushing out of the room to tell everybody what he had done. The more considered recollection was of 'a childish, cowardly thing to do. I just wanted someone to put their arms around me and care.'

Whatever Elton's requisites in the sphere of love and attention in the year before he publicly admitted bi-sexuality, his physical and emotional health had again been battered in a way which suggested that the lessons of 1974 had not been heeded.

The benefits of the period of rest occasioned by the cancellation of last year's spring tour had been offset by the resultant schedule.

To comply with the stipulations of his contract with Dick James Music, two LPs had been recorded – *Captain Fantastic* and *Rock Of The Westies*. The greatest hits album had rescued him from a third long-playing commitment. Naturally, time had to be put aside to write the songs for these projects.

As for concert work, the massive autumn American tour played to more fans than other top-line artists would encounter over a period of years. Returning home for the Christmas dates at Hammersmith, the new year offered no respite, heralding further European and Stateside obligations.

Allied to the stress caused by the band departures, rehearsing the arrivals, and concern over how the new formation would be received, there appeared adequate basis for Elton's inner turmoil, quite apart from any personal problems he may have been experiencing.

Contrasting with the negative consensus on the Wembley gig, Elton continued to blaze a dollar-strewn path on the American market. At MCA Records, executives experienced Christmas and Thanksgiving combined as *Captain Fantastic* made history by débuting on the Billboard album charts at number one, a feat later repeated by *Rock Of The Westies*.

Time magazine allotted him the space normally designated to a Presidential candidate to explain to its readers the performing credo of an artist said to be already responsible for the sale of sixty million records worldwide.

'Since I'm not your rangy rock idol in skinny leather pants, I wear flamboyant clothes,' Elton began. 'People shouldn't take the clothes and the dyed hair too seriously. Honestly, it's just a joke. I'm affectionately parodying the rock 'n' roll business by saying: "Here it is. Let's all have a laugh and enjoy ourselves."

'I didn't start enjoying life until I was twenty-one so I'm living through my teenage period now.'

'Someone Saved My Life Tonight', a minor hit in Britain, demon-strated Elton's sales power in America by reaching number four in the Billboard singles listings.

A deal agreed in 1974 with MCA, reportedly guaranteed him eight million dollars in royalties over a five-year period. The contract was considered no great risk by the company – and rightly so in the wake of *Captain Fantastic*, MCA expecting to recoup its investment well within the timespan. On behalf of the struggling artist, John Reid was quoted as suggesting that eight million was a low dollar estimate.

Augmenting Elton's Stateside infallibility, Rocket (USA) signing, Neil Sedaka, preceded 'Island Girl' at number one on Billboard with 'Bad Blood'. Elton himself featured on the single as harmony vocalist; Nigel Olsson was on drums.

Sedaka's renaissance as a potent force spoke volumes about the stagnation of the music industry prior to the first spiky stirrings of punk.

Ex-Beatles, extant Stones and Who projects individual and collect-ive were gold-plated guarantees in America. Across the Atlantic, the days of glamrock and teenybop were, mercifully, numbered. In the vanguard of the latter manifestation were the tacky and tartan Bay City Rollers, strong candidates for the most fortuitous ever recipients of successive British number one singles.

Five years at the top had guaranteed Elton a hierarchical place in any rock hall of fame. But considering his disparate outside interests, how strong was the determination to remain in the limelight?

'I can only do this for so long you know,' he confessed. 'I don't see myself singing "Crocodile Rock" when I'm thirty-four.'

Although his thirty-fourth birthday was still six years away, the signs of battle fatigue were evident.

He talked of a potential involvement in English sport beyond his burgeoning association with Watford Football Club. 'Much of the sports administration in England is outdated and the facilities are terrible. I want to try to change all that.' Yet, as always, he ended up surprising himself as much as simultaneously embarrassing his detractors in the media.

The Troubadour in Los Angeles remained a talisman for Elton. When making his American début there back in 1970, he had – in common with other emergent talents – signed a contract promising further appearances.

In view of the undreamt of reaction, Elton's management baulked at the prospect of him having to return there when a second tour was hastily assembled to capitalize on his breakthrough.

An allegedly substantial circumvention fee was paid to satisfy the aspirations of both the performer and the Troubadour ownership.

But to commemorate the fifth anniversary of his Stateside conquest Elton returned to the scene of his triumph for a series of shows in aid of the Jules Stein Eye Institute at the University of California.

The Troubadour could hardly be described as a glitzy joint. Yet the first night audience had to cough up 250 dollars a head for the privilege of witnessing a special birthday performance. Still, to such patrons of the arts as Cher, Ringo Starr, Mae West, Tony Curtis and Hugh Hefner, the admission price hardly broke the bank.

The other shows set the lucky ticket holders back a mere 25 bucks, a veritable bargain, considering that over 100,000 people were unsuccessful in their applications.

In every conceivable sense, the Troubadour had never seen anything like it. Only months previously, the talk had been of impending closure through poor support – although the word was that the rumours had been cultivated by the venue's shrewd boss, Doug Weston, in the hope of attracting more business.

Now such was the chaos caused by the crowds that the police had to barricade Santa Monica Boulevard to exclude traffic, inconveniencing residents endeavouring to reach their homes.

Inside the venue, Elton was on top form. The gala opening out of the way, he informed subsequent audiences: 'It was all right playing to the seventy-year-olds but tonight is going to be even better.'

Thanks were expressed to the departed Murray and Olsson and special tribute paid to his songwriting partner during a chronological trip through memory lane. All told, the benefit gigs raised an estimated 150,000 dollars for the eye clinic.

Weeks previously, Elton had been voted the world's top rocker at a major American music awards. And the next single, 'Island Girl', was released a week too late in the States to keep the star on course in challenging a record established by Pat Boone.

When 'Someone Saved My Life Tonight' slipped out of the Billboard top 100 in October, it ended a two-year period during which Elton boasted at least one single in the listings every week.

After a good deal of prevarication, 'Island Girl' was finally selected as the first single to be culled from Rock Of The Westies, the competing claims of 'Dan Dare (Pilot Of The Future)' having been rejected after volatile debate between Elton and John Reid.

A likely sounding candidate for an Hawaiian Tourist Board promotional campaign, 'Island Girl' was the third American chart topper from the last four singles. In truth, it was a so-so track from one of Elton's weaker albums.

Recorded at Caribou with the new band in the aftermath of Wembley, the guilt-ridden star decided to dedicate it to his former bassist and drummer, who must have wondered what to make of the inclusion of a song titled 'Hard Luck Story'. So, too, did the press, when attempting to ascertain the credentials of its mysterious composing team, Ann Orson and Carte Blanche.

Orson and Blanche were none other than Taupin and John, the in-joke pseudonym being again utilized the following year on 'Don't Go Breaking My Heart'.

Of the rest of *Westies*, 'I Feel Like A Bullet (In The Gun Of Robert Ford)' was an archetypal Elton ballad, and extremely welcome among bland company. Released as a double A-side with the rather contrived rocker, 'Grow Some Funk Of Your Own' (for which Davey Johnstone shared the writing credits), it was soon comfortably ensconced in the American top twenty. While the British record-buying public displayed greater resistance, there was hardly cause for anxiety.

All the major US trade papers announced Elton as the best-selling male artist of the year. The hits' compilation and *Captain Fantastic* each sold in prodigious quantities, the latter still high in the charts when *Rock Of The Westies* entered at number one.

Pete Townshend equated Elton's phenomenal popularity Stateside with his stature as the only artist in the rock sphere whom middle-class Americans would permit their offspring to adulate.

Similarly questioned about his inestimable asset, John Reid firstly attributed Elton's success to frequent touring and numerous public appearances before deigning to focus on the music. A crucial addendum was that the person in the street could identify with him: 'I think they see him as an amiable, very talented eccentric – which is what he is.'

Reid was speaking during what must rank as the ultimate office party.

In a typically philanthropic gesture, Elton funded a sybaritic package holiday for some 130 beneficiaries. The lucky family, friends, staff and journalists assembled at Heathrow to board a Los Angeles bound aircraft which had been chartered by the star. Another traveller was Russell Harty, there to record the events for posterity with a London Weekend Television team.

Having each been presented with a gift bag of holiday appurtenances – among which was a small camera – the tourists could picture an enticing itinerary.

Billeted at the Beverly Hills Holiday Inn, their week culminated in a dual highlight. On both Saturday and Sunday, the party was split in two. Half the revellers were taken to a marina where Elton's birthday present to John Reid – a 65 foot boat called *Madman* – was berthed. The remainder got to see Elton and his revised band give a more competent stadium performance than at Wembley five months earlier, at the home of the Los Angeles Dodgers baseball team.

The most rapturously received costume change revealed the star in a glittering Dodgers' outfit. The number on the back was one and there were none in the stadium prepared to question the sentiment during the course of a rousing three-and-a-half hour set.

Billie Jean King's augmenting of the chorus line on 'The Bitch Is Back' gave Bernie his most admired stage partner since Lennon at Madison Square Garden. Elton's special guests enjoyed themselves immeasurably.

Kiki Dee was on the West Coast at the time and thus not a bona fide member of the package trip. Yet joining up with the touring party, she was touched by the pleasure resultant from the star's generosity.

'The really nice thing about it was that they took people who didn't have the means to jet off for a week in LA. My sister was among the party and I think Bernie even invited his gardener.

'I remember going to Disneyland and seeing the Rocket accountants wandering around in a trance trying to figure out what was going on. But it was a lovely gesture, showing the style that Elton and John Reid have. They know how to live.'

Before a note was played in anger, Elton had already left an indelible mark on Tinsel Town. On 23 October at midday at Graumann's Chinese Theatre, Hollywood Boulevard, Elton's star was laid into the ground alongside those of John Wayne, Paul Newman and other entertainment luminaries.

Resplendent in a sequinned bowler and chartreuse ensemble, the recipient of the honour took it all in his stride. After all, it was Elton John Week in Los Angeles. 'Captain Fantastic' had passed from legend to festival.

With other accomplishments including participation in a major charity tennis tournament and playing truant from the Caribou Ranch to join the Rolling Stones on stage in Denver, 1975 had been the year of Fat Reg from Pinner.

After a truly momentous twelve months, it was only to be expected that 1976 would pall in comparison.

An open secret had been made official with the announcement that Elton would record for Rocket after a final album had fulfilled his contractual obligations to Dick James Music.

Less coverage was devoted to the agreement of a licensing deal with EMI in Britain, Rocket's domestic distribution having been previously handled by Island.

Despite the lift-off given to the infant label by Neil Sedaka in America, things had remained static on the home front.

Stackridge, Maldwyn Pope, Longdancer, the Hudson Brothers and others were conspicuously lacking in commercial worth; Davey Johnstone and Nigel Olsson had proved talents of limited appeal outside the confines of the Elton John Band.

It was really Kiki Dee against the world, and she was of the steadfast opinion that Elton's value to the label as an artist far outstripped his publicity benefits as a figurehead. 'Things were ticking over, but there had been few hits. Rocket really needed the boost of an Elton John album.'

The boost was to come in double measure in the autumn. But first things first.

Elton went public with plans for an arduous British tour in spring, the centrepiece of which would be concerts at the 17,000 capacity Earl's Court arena in London. The now standard practice of benefitting charities would be maintained and, reflecting the star's prime non-musical preoccupation, the proceeds from the Earl's Court gigs were earmarked for the Sports Aid Foundation.

Tickets sold at a pace commensurate with past American concerts, engendering the normal consequence – the addition of extra performances to an extensive list of dates.

The tour went under the by-line of 'Louder than Concorde – but not quite as pretty', a theme allegedly of Royal descent. The authoritative word was that, taking tea with Princess Margaret, Elton was told in jest that his piano playing registered higher on the decibel scale than Britain's fastest passenger aircraft.

Whether true or apocryphal, it made a distinctive motif for the jackets sported by Elton's party during what was his first major British itinerary for three years.

The 1974 programme had been cancelled in the wake of the trouble in New Zealand and the tension at the Caribou sessions. Aside from the Hammersmith Christmas dates and the odd charity or Watford benefit, the only concert of note in the intervening period had been the Wembley Stadium gig – and Elton was anxious to show off the new band in a more favourable light to his home fans.

Indisputably, the mission was accomplished, the band proving on top form from the opening night in Leeds. For the London dates, Elton utilized his American experience to provide an object lesson in how to give the optimum performance in a cavernous auditorium.

The shape of things to come was previewed at Earl's Court by the use of a thirty-foot screen above the stage affording a better view of the proceedings for those less advantageously positioned. Conversely, Elton could only envisage a limited future for the second incarnation of the Elton John Band.

A lowly English soccer team had given his life new perspective.

11

'The kind of age group that were playing guitar
when the Beatles started now go to football
matches' (Elton John, 1971)

One of the few pleasures shared between Elton and his
father were the occasional trips to watch Watford Football
Club, then one of the league's cinderella outfits. While the
schoolboy Reg Dwight may have been prohibited from playing
football in the garden, he at least managed to indulge a passion for
sport vicariously on the club's Vicarage Road terraces.

Furthermore he could exhibit family pride in the bitter-sweet
legend of a member of the Dwight clan who did grace the game's
biggest stage. Cousin, Roy Dwight, earned a perverse place in football
folklore when playing for Nottingham Forest, one of the country's
leading clubs. He turned out for Forest in the 1959 FA Cup Final against
Luton, scored the first goal in a 2–1 victory, but then broke his leg, an
injury which ended his career in the game's top flight.

Although a famous Watford giant-killing FA Cup run had been
ended by a star-studded Chelsea team at the semi-final stage,
Wembley was a pipedream to all at Vicarage Road, save for those who
deserted the footballing backwater for the north London grounds of
perennial finalists, Spurs and Arsenal.

More realistic were annual pilgrimages to such soccer shrines as
Stockport and Hartlepool, interspersed with the odd false dawn of
promotion.

In the early 1970s, the game still maintained something of a cloth
cap image. Thus the concept of one of the world's most outrageous
rock performers joining the board of directors of a lower league club
seemed fanciful.

Yet galvanized by an interview with a local journalist, Elton rose to the challenge in the mode of the true iconoclast. At first the involvement was in the nature of testing the water – an appearance at the unlikely venue of Watford Top Rank in a testimonial event for long-serving player, Duncan Welbourne.

It wasn't just his dedication which endeared Elton to the Vicarage Road hierarchy. With his recollections of Watford when the team wore blue and tales of players who all but the diehards had forgotten, he knew as much about the club as any of them – if not more.

Elton graduated from a vice-presidency to a directorship in 1974, the same year that a record Vicarage Road crowd cheered him in an on-field role – headlining the concert fund-raiser with Rod Stewart.

When he succeeded Jim Bonser as chairman in 1976, he nevertheless inherited a fourth division club in a parlous financial state. Reacting to the news that Watford owed the bank nearly £100,000 and had been loaned nearly £150,000 by directors in recent years, Elton made it clear that despite his spiralling fortune, he had no intention of being regarded as a meal ticket.

'This is not just a happy little bandwagon with me just picking up the bills,' he declared. 'The board are working hard to make the club pay for itself. If Elton John being chairman puts 2,000 on the gate I shall be pleased. But I don't believe in gimmicks.'

Equally, Elton was anxious to dispel any notion that his music commitments would render him little more than an absent figurehead.

'I don't intend missing many matches either home or away because I've reached the stage in my career where I don't need to chase all over the world as much as I used to.' Sceptics national and local dismissed his interest as transitory.

Yet he was as good as his word. In later years, a desire to fly back from concert tours abroad for crucial first division or European fixtures reflected the understandable behaviour of a proud, conscientious and wealthy chairman. But the same sacrifices were made for bread-and-butter games at the league's lowest level.

Starting in the manner he intended to continue, the star flew back from an American tour to watch a league match at Cambridge the following day as the 1976–77 league season got under way.

Although all the first campaign brought was a familiarity with some of the country's less fashionable stadia, Elton was hooked. 'Suddenly, I was back in the atmosphere I hade loved as a kid and involved with people,' he enthused.

'When I came into the club I was so tired. I didn't want to do anything except rest for a couple of years. But I can't sit around the house doing nothing and Watford gave me the opportunity to do something different. It has been a fantastic experience.'

Actually, save for the club failing to win promotion, the first season had provided Elton with the perfect introduction to football chairmanship. His rapport with the Vicarage Road faithful had been embellished, he was on good terms with the staff and while the subject of ribald chants at away grounds, the abuse was almost affectionate in football terms. Moreover, if other fourth division chairmen harboured qualms about opening the boardroom drinks cabinet to an extrovert rock 'n' roller, the majority hid it well.

Watford forward, Keith Mercer, who had been at the club since Elton's initial tentative involvement, remembers how the players quickly established an understanding with the star.

'Firstly, we knew him by the high heels and green hair. Elton was mainly around at matches, but also came training. From the outset, he was very approachable. I remember that when I was twenty I was trying to grow a tash, without too much success. Elton said: "I'll show you what it's like" and by the end of the week had a full facial growth. I said to him: "When you can grow that on your face, it's a shame you can't do the same on your head." '

On another occasion, the star brought Rod Stewart along for a practice session and they played on different sides.

'While Rod was very good, as befits someone who almost took up the game, Elton was not too clever. He knew what he wanted to do but his body wouldn't let him.'

'There's nothing wrong with going to bed with somebody of your own sex. I think everybody is bisexual to a certain degree. It's not a bad thing to be.'

So said Elton to Cliff Jahr of *Rolling Stone* magazine in probably the most revealing interview he has ever given. 'Elton's frank talk – the lonely love life of a superstar' was the influential journal's cover story for 7 October 1976.

Jahr was the first media man to confront the star about the rumours surrounding his sexuality. In response to sympathetic questioning, Elton confided: 'I would love to have an affair, I crave to be loved.

'I'm just going through a stage where any sign of affection would be welcome on a sexual level. I'd rather fall in love with a woman . . . But I really don't know. I haven't met anybody that I would like to settle down with – of either sex.'

As the interview progressed, so Elton relaxed, palpably relieved that the matter had finally been brought into the public domain. But amidst a fascinating insight into the surprisingly lonely life of the world's top-selling artist came the quote that would be remembered long after all else: 'I just think people should be very free with sex – they should draw the line at goats.'

In the contemporary climate, sub-editors the world over would be on cloud nine composing garish headlines. In 1976, the Sex Pistols swearing on a local news programme was a natural lead story. But a confession of bisexuality posed an editorial dilemma.

Thus, the more sensitive of the British press tactfully ignored the *Rolling Stone* interview . . . But not all.

Ironically, the story broke as Elton was fulfilling his Watford duties by accompanying the team to a fourth division fixture at, of all places, Rochdale, having confessed to Cliff Jahr: It's going to be terrible with my football club. It's so hetero, it's unbelievable.'

The sports staff were relegated to a back seat as the gossip writers were dispatched to try to elicit any further true confessions. What they got was something of an anti-climax.

Having fielded questions on present girl/boy friends with one word negatives, Elton added: 'Seriously, all this fuss doesn't bother me. But I do feel sorry for the team. They will have to suffer a lot of abuse.'

Although this was true to an extent, it was primarily Elton the away crowds would bait. As an illustration, a typical Rochdale attendance of 1,760 spent ninety minutes calling his manhood into question. However, there was a more striking blow to his pride. Watford lost 3–1.

Aside from being an increasing target of uncomplimentary chants from the terraces, there was little perceivable change in the British public's affection towards Elton.

While distaste is widely expressed when the peccadillos of political figures are exposed, deviances from the accepted sexual norm are tolerated almost unquestioningly in theatrical entertainers.

Indicative of public support was the reaction of the Watford team. Said Keith Mercer: 'We were all tarred with the same brush by opposing fans, which wasn't very nice. But the revelations didn't change our views about him.'

In marked difference, the post-interview response in America tended more towards the hostile – 'you know, calling me a faggot. And yet America's supposed to be the great liberated free-minded society. Which, of course, it isn't.'

Though acknowledging that there was no way he could envisage a return to the heady sales figures of 1975 and before, Elton still latterly declared that the interview proved to his commercial detriment in the US.

'Everyone goes love and peace man, but it'll never happen because hatred is rammed into their kids by parents – and hate makes much more money.'

The *Rolling Stone* confessions were certainly no surprise to Sheila Farebrother, who had learnt of her son's sexual leanings through a telephone call five years previously. 'I was upset at first,' she later admitted. 'But I think it was a very brave thing for him to do. I would still like to think he can find some kind of happiness with a male or female – I don't care.'

Other stars praised Elton's openness while a poll conducted by a music paper showed fans unconcerned about what he did off stage and outside recording hours. Future criticism should be confined solely to his music, the respondents agreed.

Kiki Dee was among friends who considered the disclosure sensible, if courageous. 'I'm sure it was a great relief to him once the article was printed. It was typical of him to follow his instincts, even if the comments were potentially risky. The climate was right for that kind of honesty.'

In fact, if Elton had consciously chosen to come clean about his private life, the timing could not have been more propitious. It was on other subjects that his public utterances were equivocal.

Whereas a year previously, he had talked excitedly about the potential of his new band, conversation now centred on a parting devoid of acrimony. 'It's silly keeping them under contract for a year because I might never work again.'

At the last of seven sell-out performances at New York's Madison Square Garden, which had set a record for the venue, the star announced: 'You won't see me for a while but I'll be back . . . someday.' Elton said he had been so touched by the reception accorded him by the MSG audiences that he broke a vow 'just for you' not to play 'Your Song' on the American tour. They didn't know, or care, that preceding crowds had been moved by the same 'spontaneous' gesture.

The consensus of press and public was that if this was an authentic farewell tour, he should do them more often. With Elton conservatively expected to gross 1.25 million dollars from the concerts, the concept was certainly not without its appeal to his financial advisers.

In celebration of the bicentennial, there were firework displays at the open-air concerts which challenged the extravagance of Elton's stage attire. A Statue of Liberty ensemble was a mainstay, while a Stars and Stripes hot-pants suit attracted considerable attention.

Memories of the bygone days of Legs Larry Smith were rekindled by the outrageous support act of Billy Connolly, described by one bemused reviewer as 'a bawdy Scottish country and western singer'. And almost by popular demand, Kiki Dee was recruited to join in the organized mayhem.

In the summer of 1976, 'a complete one-off single with Kiki' had finally given Elton a British number one.

'Don't Go Breaking My Heart' emanated from a day the star had spent idly messing around in the studio on an electric piano.

Hitting upon the title line, he summarily rang up Bernie in Barbados, issuing the simple instruction: 'Write a duet'. His songwriting partner was temporarily flummoxed – a song for two represented virgin territory.

Yet he came back with the ingredients for a perfect pop song – on this occasion with Elton's lyrical assistance – a worthy counterpart to the Motown duets featuring Marvin Gaye that the star so admired.

Kiki Dee revealed that she and Elton had discussed the possibility of a duet at intervals during their musical relationship. 'We both adored the Marvin Gaye and Tammi Terrell records and wondered why no one was doing that sort of thing anymore. But we had our respective commitments and there was the complication that we were on different labels.'

The latter obstacle having been removed, Elton recorded his vocals in March at Eastern Sound in Toronto, as a diversion from the sessions for the forthcoming *Blue Moves* double album.

'We actually did the song together in London,' Kiki revealed. 'But for whatever reason, it was decided to stick with Elton's Canadian vocal track.'

Credited to that well-known songwriting team of 'Orson and Blanche' and produced by Gus Dudgeon, the record topped the charts in Britain and the States for six and four weeks respectively. When it reached pole position in Britain, Elton reacted as though Watford had won the FA Cup, ringing all and sundry with the news. (To this day, he has yet to achieve a solo number one in his country of birth.)

Paradoxically, having been considered within Rocket as a boost for Kiki's career, the single did as much, if not more for Elton, selling prodigiously in what for him were new territories. What better welcome to the roster of his own label?

After bidding America a temporary adieu amid glittering spectacle, Elton returned to Britain to give a performance solitary in all its aspects.

Coinciding with the September launch of *Blue Moves*, Elton gave a concert at the Edinburgh Playhouse.

Shorn of all musical and visual aids – with the exception of Kiki waiting in the wings for the inevitable finale – Elton reverted to the traditional niche of the singer–songwriter. Just a man and his piano.

As he gained in composure and confidence, the audience and viewers (Scottish Television was providing live transmission), gained rare insight into the fears and frustrations of a superstar.

'Us so-called megastars have to be brought down to earth,' he declared at one point. 'That's why I'm going off the road – to re-evaluate. People have to make four phone calls before they're allowed to talk to me . . . That kind of thing gets irritating.'

From jittery beginnings, without the safety net of the band, the performance had instilled a reviving measure of pride and confidence in the artist. Yet in contrast to past triumphs, further concerts were not the natural consequence.

Blue Moves was again evidence of artistic bravery. Starting off on your label with an extended set hardly equates with safety-first. A possible explanation was that Bernie and Elton were irrevocably accustomed to supplying the material for the two LPs per annum stipulated in the contract with Dick James. A more plausible script depicted a guilty Elton feeling that those who had purchased the final DJM LP were owed something extra.

Though live albums rarely strike the listener as wholly satisfactory, there are good examples of the genre. Here And There – featuring highlights of the 1974 concerts at the Royal Festival Hall and Madison Square Garden – was patently not one of these.

A low point in terms both of quality and sales, Here And There alluded to a less than harmonious parting of the ways. Elton was to allege that DJM was offered Blue Moves in return for the destruction of the live tapes.

Notorious for their commercial risks, live LPs are eschewed wherever possible by record companies. So, in theory, it was barely conceivable that DJM would have snubbed the offer of a fresh studio product in recompense for a small fire.

This is confirmed by former executives of the company who suggested that had new recordings been proffered as part of a barter deal, corporate mountains would have been moved to ensure the transaction's smooth implementation.

In the light of the legal suit brought belatedly against his former employer, it is relevant to contemplate the tolerance displayed by Dick James during Elton's final, fractious months at DJM.

His opinion was that Elton was virtually unmanageable during the Captain Fantastic period. The closer to the conclusion of the contract, the more delicate the relationship between star and label became.

Dick James understood Elton wishing to devote more of his time and energies to Rocket, and reluctantly acknowledged that he would desire the next studio release to appear on his own label.

DJM didn't want Here And There any more than the public. An option was to seek legal redress, the decision was to compromise.

When Dylan's (by then) legendary Basement Tapes were put out in vinyl form by CBS in 1975, the vaults of Dick James Music were searched for any unreleased nuggets from past Elton John sessions.

A dozen likely contenders were discovered – some said to be of exemplary quality – and discussions were held as to the feasibility of compiling them as the final DJM LP.

The anguished consensus was to stick with *Here And There*, albeit with a stack of reservations. It was unarguable that ardent fans would have jumped at the opportunity to purchase a collection of unreleased studio tracks. Even casual admirers would have found such a compilation more enticing than a set of live versions of material already possessed.

But Dick James, among others, had no wish to be accused of putting out a record which might be construed as harmful to Elton's career.

Retrospectively, the company realized its folly. Nothing could have caused greater detriment to the star's reputation than *Here And There*. The sound quality was indifferent, and as Elton himself conceded, nervousness about John Lennon's impending guest slot negated much of what went before at the Madison Square Garden concert.

Furthermore, DJM decided not to pursue the possibility of including the three Lennon collaborations from the Garden show on the LP (the songs appeared on a special maxi-single, with the consent of EMI). The prime consideration was that *Here and There*, for all its faults, should be seen wholly as an Elton John product.

If DJM were unhappy at the situation, MCA in America were furious, Elton being the company's eight million dollar man.

Under the prevailing circumstances, it was difficult to apportion any great blame on DJM in trying to squeeze the utmost from their incalculable asset by finally releasing 'Bennie And The Jets' as a single. It failed to match its American success, peaking outside the BBC top thirty.

Analysis of *Blue Moves* shows that Rocket had much the better of the contractual bargain. Underneath a welter of guest appearances from orchestras, choirs and half of Crosby, Stills, Nash and Young lays a largely convincing product.

Previewing the album in a spring interview, Bernie Taupin promised 'uptempo disco stompers, Bob Marley-type tracks, Spinners-type tracks (and) a few instrumentals. There's a lot of very downer songs too – suicide material – but good at the same time.'

In this instance, it was Bernie who had cause for the suicidal tendencies in the wake of the painful estrangement from his first wife. The most acclaimed of the morose love songs was 'Sorry Seems To Be

The Hardest Word', with Elton once more in the unaccustomed guise of co-lyricist.

Otherwise, attention focussed on the inspiration behind two tracks. 'Idol', a song about a star on the wane, was assumed to have Presley as a reference point. That recognized, Elton described it as a salutary warning about his own career if he trod an erroneous future path.

Superficially, 'If There's A God In Heaven (What's He Waiting For?)' was construed as a savage indictment of poverty and human suffering. Yet shortly after the album's release, Elton was quoted as claiming the song to be a parody.

'I said to Taupin: "Let's do a song like that with a really tacky lyric and see if we can get away with it." It is a ridiculous song deliberately.' Meanwhile, he produced another Kiki Dee album and also an LP by China, something of an old boys collective, as the band featured Davey Johnstone and James Newton Howard.

As now well established, his production partner was Clive Franks.

Another graduate of the Dick James organization, Clive had progressed from messenger boy to engineer by way of cutting and tape operator.

His involvement with Elton dated right back to *Empty Sky*, on which his credit was 'tape operator and whistling'. A brief period with Island Studios – during which he worked with Jimi Hendrix and Eric Clapton – presaged a return to DJM in the elevated capacity of studio manager and chief engineer.

Elton's penchant for surrounding himself with familiar faces had prompted Clive's return to his retinue in 1972. Dissatisfied with the sound quality at his concerts, Elton called Clive from Amsterdam to take over as sound man. History shows Elton as being a difficult man to refuse.

Soon to inherit the mantle of Gus Dudgeon without as much as a bloodless coup, Clive was sincerely grateful to Elton for instilling confidence in his own abilities.

From an artist's viewpoint, Kiki Dee described Clive and Elton as the perfect production combination. 'I think my opening Rocket LP was the first time that Clive and Elton had worked together as producers. It was a creative success because it was a team effort. Clive is such a good sound engineer, Elton exudes confidence in the studio. A performer understands a performer, appreciating what motivates them.

'Of course, being good friends, Clive and Elton could relieve any tension with humour. They were always bursting into fits of giggles.'

Clive also acknowledged the benefits to both production parties. 'Through Elton I'm learning about relating to artists while he is gaining technical knowledge.'

Having rapidly acquired a first hit in 'Amoureuse', the production team worked with an expanding roster of artists under the trading name of Frank N. Stein, Elton's behind-the-scenes equivalent of Blanche and Orson.

In the studio, Clive felt their relationship had since progressed to the point of telepathy. 'Each of us knows when the other is having a bad time and tries to lift him out of it.

'We never disagree. He'll make a suggestion like: "What would a guitar solo sound like backwards?" And while I'm trying it out, Elton will do something like playing backgammon. Sometimes his suggestions seem strange. But more often than not he's right.'

T he Watford FC chairman's end-of-season assessment for 1976–77 was that the club had the potential to be a second division outfit within five years. However, future perceptions required positive revision after the summer signing of the man who was to exert a seminal influence on the star's life.

Graham Taylor gave up an opportunity of managership with first division West Bromwich Albion to sign a five-year contract with the Hertfordshire club in May 1977.

A fellow young idealist in a sport stifled by outmoded thinking, Taylor had served an impressive managerial apprenticeship with third division Lincoln. It was typical of Elton's desire for the best in all aspects of life that he was engaged at a salary of £25,000, making him one of Britain's highest paid football bosses.

Taylor's accomplishments in his first season in charge went a long way to repaying his chairman, and the Watford board, who had vetoed Elton's earlier plans to install former England captain, Bobby Moore, in the manager's chair. As in his musical life, Elton was learning from his mistakes – and he was a voracious student.

Watford clinched promotion to the third division with a win at Bournemouth and ensured the title with another victory at Scunthorpe a few days later, with Elton travelling to matches from the States as the City commuter would catch the 7.40 to Waterloo. When Brentford also earned elevation to a higher echelon with a draw at Vicarage Road, the West London club's vice-president – keyboard wizard, Rick Wakeman – afforded Elton an additional celebration opportunity.

More schoolboy than megastar when he congratulated his triumphant team in the changing room, he cut an unintentionally comic figure, an outsized checked cap covering a recent hair transplant. By now immersed in soccer jargon, the requisite quote came easily: 'Promotion again, that's the target for next season. There's no point in consolidating. You've got to be positive in football.'

With great prescience, Graham Taylor added: 'We don't know the full potential of this club yet. But we're on course.'

Elton's involvement was at times a mixed blessing. Players who might normally have rejected a move to a lower league club were enticed by the high profile Watford now boasted. Conversely, other teams tended to up the asking price if bids for a star were received from Vicarage Road. Explained Graham Taylor: 'They expect Elton to sign a cheque, cash deals and no hire purchases. We can't operate like that.'

The benefits, though, far outweighed the drawbacks. The town was proud of its team – as attendances reflected – and accepted Elton warts and all. The doubters could be converted.

Said Keith Mercer: 'He had a tremendously impressive general knowledge about football. I remember that one night the supporters' club ran a quiz – directors versus players versus supporters. People could just not believe how many questions Elton got right.'

For his part, the fledgling football supremo was enveloped in a Roy of the Rovers dream. So in awe was he of Taylor's assistant, Bertie Mee – who managed the double-winning Arsenal team of 1971 – that it was a struggle to put the relationship on a first name footing.

'We were stars to him as he was a star to us,' remarked Keith Mercer. Though not to the point where the chairman refrained from motivating the players before a fixture as he might his fellow musicians before a concert.

'Before a game, he was always in the dressing room, geeing the lads up. Just his presence made us feel good.'

Initially, the relationship between chairman and players was conducted on an informal basis. Conversations were on first-name terms, a quiet word invariably ensured concert tickets and a new Elton release would guarantee the incongruous sight of a chauffeured Rolls-Royce arriving at the ground laden with boxes of records. Watford apprentices were summoned to assist the beleaguered driver with the delivery.

On the arrival of Graham Taylor, however, things reverted to a more formal level.

According to Keith Mercer, the record deliveries continued. 'But we had to call him "Mr Chairman" instead of Elton. And if we went to see him in concert, it was as a coach party, rather than individuals. Elton accepted this, respecting Graham Taylor's judgement.

'They were like business partners in the very best sense, becoming good friends as well. Graham could say to Elton: "This is my team and I don't want you in the dressing room today." And Elton would comply.

'I remember Elton being very excited when we won the fourth division, promising to take the players on a pre-season tour of Australia. Graham Taylor asked him what he would then do if we won the third – or even the second. He accepted the argument. In fact, I think we ended up going to Scotland!'

There were times when the worlds of football and show business merged. Elton coerced team members into displaying diverse vocal talents on the album, A *Single Man*. The end product was quite acceptable although producer, Clive Franks, still relives the horror of keeping the less tutored voices out of range in the studio.

In the main, Elton was grateful for the down to earth attitudes of the football fraternity. He readily credits Graham Taylor as a steadying influence in times of crisis by showing intolerance of behaviour showbiz associates would just let pass. If Elton turned up on match days dressed in a manner unbefitting to a club chairman, it would not go unremarked. Similarly, Taylor had taken the star to task for excessive drinking. The honesty of the relationship partly explained one of the longest running football partnerships – it ended on amicable terms in 1987 – and Elton's most productive professional liaison apart from his work with that other son of Lincolnshire, Bernie Taupin.

Whatever cosmetic adjustments in the chairman-player relationship implemented by Graham Taylor on taking charge at Vicarage Road, one social engagement remained unaltered – its cancellation would likely have resulted in mutiny among the Watford squad.

Once a year, Elton threw open his home to the team and officials with their respective wives, girlfriends and children.

Said Keith Mercer: 'The players really looked forward to it. There was champagne and caviar and the pool was great for the kids. He was the perfect host.

'One of the nicest things was that Elton made a point of remembering the names of wives and children, so that it was all really informal.'

By the Graham Taylor era, Elton had forsaken the pleasures of Virginia Water for Woodside, a sumptuous abode in Old Windsor, purchased for in the region of £400,000.

According to legend, the mansion was built by Henry VIII for one of his mistresses. If so, there was ample room to hide the concubine in the event of a visit by an intrusive wife.

A feature of its grounds was a vineyard, a talking point of the present interior a cinema with full-length screen. True to his character in *Tommy*, he was addicted to pinball machines, an enthusiasm reflected in a huge games room.

The decor was enhanced by Elton's fine taste in antiques and paintings, a Rembrandt among them. But in the style of a true vinyl junkie, attention was first given to finding a suitable resting place for his record library, said to compare favourably with all but the BBC's own collection.

A captivated Kiki Dee said of the home: 'It is just so full of wonderful things – pieces, paintings – that there is almost too much to appreciate.

'The library is basically a huge room stacked with little winding corridors of records. Elton listens to anything. He is very aware of everything that is going on musically and can tell instantly whether or not he likes an album.'

Kiki remembered that when newly-signed to Rocket, Elton casually mentioned that he was escorting her record shopping. Her expectation was of a handful of carefully chosen albums. She arrived home with seventy. But that was nothing. When in America, Elton always allowed himself ample time for a depletion raid on the prodigious stocks of the famous Tower Records.

Personal assistant, Andy Hill, was shell-shocked during an inaugural expedition: 'We went to Tower Records in Los Angeles, shooting up and down the pathways between the various record sections. Elton literally whizzed through the store chucking any he hadn't got into the basket.' The volume of purchases was less awe-inspiring than the manner. Elton treated record stores as the rest of the world utilized supermarkets.

Although a lover of Black music – he always craved a group like the Stylistics for the Rocket roster – Elton's tastes were catholic, at this stage encompassing Stevie Winwood, the Alan Parsons Project and Linda Ronstadt, a periodic visitor to his West Coast home.

There were not enough hours in the day for Elton to play all of his recorded acquisitions. But he endeavoured to acquaint himself with as much as possible, whether at home, at work or in transit.

One of Andy Hill's tasks was to ensure that when Elton was based in hotels, his suite was fitted with a full hi-fi system. Another essential creature comfort for the star on his travels was an electric piano.

If generous to himself, Elton continued a giving propensity towards others. To his family and closest friends, a gift for that unthinkingly special occasion might, at the upper limit, run to a Rolls-Royce or Rembrandt etching.

In no sense was he an easy touch, rather an inordinately wealthy man with a lavishly idosyncratic way of rewarding loyalty or celebrating friendship. Certainly, there was no shortage of gold and platinum discs for distribution.

On a relatively mundane level, staff could find themselves benefitting from an impulsive gesture if providing the escort party on a shopping trip.

For example, Andy Hill: 'We'd be in Bloomingdales and he'd say: "Oh, I never buy you anything." Then he would pick up a pile of silk shirts and a couple of suits and say: "Here you are." Just like that.'

Sheila Farebrother recalled a touching example of her son's philanthropy taken to excess. Remarking to Elton that she needed a new compact, Sheila was rendered speechless by the gift of a £1,500 model from Cartier – an altogether too exotic accessory for everyday use.

A US correspondent who accompanied Elton on a shopping expedition to Cartier in 1975 reported the following litany of token gifts for band members and staff: four briefcases, three gold cigarette lighters, a necklace and a bracelet. Dissatisfied with that little haul, he proceeded to a nearby art gallery to divest himself of a few more thousand pounds.

Two years later, Cartier hastily called up a dozen employees from its New York Fifth Avenue store for a little unexpected Sunday overtime.

Having been informed that Elton wanted to go shopping, the store's executives decreed that he was just too good a customer to disappoint.

Cartier's revenue from this one-man spree was £30,000 and the majority of the purchases were destined for others.

A month later, all staff of Rocket Records and John Reid Enterprises received an unexpected Christmas bonus – a Cartier watch.

The festive season was also the cue for another of Elton's annual footballing engagements – the Watford players' Christmas party.

Each year, Elton would bring along a celebrity figure to provide the entertainment and Keith Mercer recalled Bob Monkhouse, Roy Castle, Ronnie Barker, Lennie Bennett and Billy Connolly during his tenure at the club.

It was goodwill to all except, temporarily, his oldest associate in the music business.

Elton and Bernie were on speaking terms, but that had been the problem.

Too rarely had they shared the same writing environment. *Captain Fantastic* had brought them together, largely due to the intensely personal nature of its contents.

It was precisely because the lyrics, for once, did relate to his life that Bernie broke the habits of a writing existence by making belated amendments. Otherwise, their work was dictated as much by the vagaries of the communications services as in the days immediately after Ray Williams brought them together.

If Elton was heading inexorably towards a period of professional estrangement from his songwriting partner, John Reid remained well entrenched in all aspects of the star's life, down even to becoming involved at Watford.

There were those in the industry who only spoke of him vituperatively, others who grudgingly admired how he and Elton had stayed together in a business marriage while divorce was being filed all around.

By his own admission, John Reid is renowned neither for a calm demeanour or an unruffled personality. A former staff member at John Reid Enterprises recounted that, on a bad day, the slightest irritation would ignite a fierce temper. A past adversary insisted that on a good day, the same would apply.

Reid has told reporters that he adhered to the principle of first exploding, then conducting the inquest.

'I yell and scream and say: "The lot of you can get out." And then I come back and talk about it and it's all OK. I can't stand it if people don't do their work.'

Nor was Elton immune from the firing line. Reid was once quoted as saying: 'My arguments with Elton get so bad that we've ended up knocking one another around. I've given him more than one black eye.'

Professional arguments have encompassed disagreement over the choice of single releases from albums and even the LP titles themselves.

'Silent Movies Talking Pictures', 'Vodka And Tonic' and 'Old Pink Eyes Is Back' were among intended album names rejected forcibly or otherwise. Far worse, Elton wanted *Rock Of The Westies* to be released as 'Bottled And Brained'.

'He's not irresponsible,' Reid opined. 'He just doesn't know where to draw the line.'

The same has been suggested of the petite Scotsman. Aside from his brush with the law in New Zealand, he made the news for whacking a San Francisco doorman over the head with a cane.

Paradoxically, the Watford players thought him polite and shy, while Kiki Dee recognized an altogether different character trait.

'Sure John is single-minded, quite volatile in a way. You have to be in his line of business and he would never have achieved so much without that hard Glaswegian edge. Yet he does have a nice gentle side. . . .'

Reid also managed Kiki and, for three years, looked after the affairs of Queen, fronted by another of rock's great characters, Freddie Mercury.

Mercury it was whose antics provided the most cherished memories for invitees and gate-crashers alike at a wild opening bash for Friends, a Covent Garden restaurant which proved one of Reid's less profitable business forays.

C ontrast the private face and public persona of Elton Hercules John. 'When I'm away from what I'm doing, I'm really quite shy,' he told an American reporter in 1976. 'I would, for instance, never go up to anyone for an autograph.'

This notion of a self-effacing showman is supported by his mother's recollection of Elton's meeting with Elvis Presley that year at a reception after an Elvis concert at the Capital Centre, Washington. Sheila Farebrother remembered her son as being 'so nervous, he didn't know what to say'.

A year later, Elton's opening announcement to a Rainbow Theatre audience including Princess Alexandra exuded the elan of the consummate master of ceremonies: 'Your royal highnesses, ladies and gentlemen and Moss Bros; good evening. I hope you've brought your choc ices with you. It's a long programme.'

A series of concerts at the north London venue ended almost a year's concert sabbatical, while also contributing handsomely to the Queen's Silver Jubilee Trust.

While the absence had hardly been idle – his dual working loyalties were with Watford and Rocket Records – the split with Bernie was undoubtedly a factor in the dearth of any new material from the singer during the year.

'I very rarely see Bernie these days,' he admitted, adding: 'Writing lyrics isn't too bad anymore, providing I get the melody first.'

An unenforced revision for concerts was Elton's experiment with a 'one-man' show – in reality, with the percussive backing of Ray Cooper, an equally manic stage performer.

For years to come, opinion would be divided between those who considered the solo gigs the perfect forum for Elton's material and critics who suggested that pared to the bone, even some of his biggest sellers translated as spartan fare. Initially, the performer himself appeared to doubt the wisdom of the drastic cut-back in stage personnel.

At the Rainbow, however, the headlines were stolen by a backstage conversation. Introduced to the star of the show, Princess Alexandra committed a stunning royal *faux pas* by inquiring: 'Do you take cocaine?'

Said Elton: 'I was so stunned, I'm not sure what I replied. She asked me how I could play for two-and-a-half hours at a stretch. Did I take some sort of drug? Did I take cocaine? I couldn't believe it.' The Princess later apologized.

The Rainbow concerts had been a watershed. 'I had to look at the situation I was in and think deeply about where I was going. Maybe things were running away a bit. I just fancied having a go on my own.'

Rather than a clarification of intent, another charity concert at the Empire Pool, Wembley, later in 1977, seemingly threw his whole performing future into question.

Elton started solo, to be subsequently augmented by Rocket colleagues, China, housing the familiar talents of Davey Johnstone and James Newton Howard.

Before the finale, Elton braced the audience for an announcement. 'I'd just like to say something. It's hard to put it into words. It's been a painful decision whether to come back on the road. I've really enjoyed tonight. But I've made a decision. This is the last one I'm going to do. There's a lot more to me than being on the road.'

Theatrical to the supposed last, Elton followed his address by playing 'Don't Let The Sun Go Down On Me'. Then Kiki Dee came on for the routine duet and, as a true surprise, Stevie Wonder – the earlier subject of a sincere dedication from the stage – was recruited from the best seats to join Elton on piano for 'Bite Your Lip'.

If it really was to be the final performance, Elton was going out in style.

Personal assistant, Andy Hill, summarized the reaction of close aides. 'The announcement was a surprise. But people who know Elton well come to expect these things – it was probably something he decided on the day of the concert.

'I'm sure the fans also knew he couldn't give up gigs for ever – that's the side of the business he really loves.'

Kiki Dee concurred. 'Retirement? Which retirement? No one thought he would give up permanently. It was just a phase. After so much success, overkill was bound to set in.'

Elton's claimed motivation for his goodbye announcement was a conviction that he was not being true to himself. Before the concert he had been in a foul mood. 'I suddenly realized that I was once again doing a big concert with truck after truck of equipment.

'I was doing things that I'd promised myself I'd never do again. I was angry with myself.'

While friends considered Elton's touring farewell to be only temporary, it was easy to understand his state of mind going into the Wembley gig.

What was the next logical move for the man who had done everything?

In seven years, Elton had recorded enough successful singles to fill two greatest hits albums – and contribute a side's worth of a third. In America, his LPs had out-sold all-comers.

He had run the performing gamut of venues, working his way from intimate halls to imposing sports stadia.

Rocket Records was well established, if not a market leader, his football team was at the dawn of an upward wave, and he could count some of the entertainment world's most famous names among his fan club.

Whether based in England or the States, he resided in fabulous luxury, explaining his travelling credo as one of living for today. 'My great theory about spending money is that life is short. I could walk out of this hotel room and the maid would come up to me and suffocate me with a great big blanket.

'I don't overspend but you can't take it with you. So many people are miserable with success. I can't be that way. I refuse to stop going out spending money and having a good time.'

After a decade with Bernie, the imminent change in his writing habits would require a signal adjustment. Yet if the next album sold in disappointing quantities, it would hardly be the end of the world. His only concern was to eschew the cabaret circuit – not the clubs he had so detested in his Bluesology days, but the casino venues where Elvis's critical reputation had foundered.

Meeting Presley, one of his heroes, in the year before his death had been a sorrowful experience for Elton.

'I wasn't really shocked when he died. When I met him he barely looked like a human being. His eyes were sunk into the back of his head. He looked gross.'

What had upset Elton even more was that he had seen the man 'first thought to be outrageous in rock 'n' roll' give a performance that was a parody of his former self.

Even in a comparatively quiet year, Elton maintained a peripatetic lifestyle. Aside from studio and concert commitments, he had made cameo appearances at Kiki Dee concerts in America, supported charity events and grasped any opportunity for involvement in sport.

In fact, he probably derived the most pleasure from one of his least documented performances. A May fixture at Brighton Football Club's Goldstone Road ground saw the Elton John XI take on a team led by former England player, Alan Mullery, in aid of the Goaldiggers charity, working for sporting facilities for youngsters.

Elton – wearing the number 7 shirt – was also in international company, his team boasting Bobby Moore, Ian St John and Jackie Charlton. Putting his Watford training to advantage, Elton scored from the penalty-spot.

A more bizarre and less publicized charity event took place in the unlikely setting of a bar in Maui during an American-based visit designated primarily for relaxation – that is, tennis.

According to Andy Hill, Elton befriended a local bar owner who was a keen supporter of Save The Whale. Almost immediately, he agreed to a concert. 'It was no more than a seaside bar and there was no advance publicity. Yet as the word got around, more and more people came. It was akin to the Pied Piper.'

Another enjoyable day served the dual purpose of dispelling rumours of intense personal acrimony between the star and his professionally estranged lyricist.

More than 5,000 people created good natured chaos in the immediate vicinity of a Manhattan record store when Elton and Bernie made a promotional appearance.

Another occasional companion during the star's period of transition raised a few eyebrows, as was probably the intention.

Now that Elton's bi-sexuality had been brought into the public domain, the tabloid press stayed hot on the trail of his private life. Therefore, assiduous choice of companions was essential, particularly on account of his burgeoning involvement in the more conservative sporting world.

The ideal companion would be female, from a monied background, inaccessible to all but the most unscrupulous news-hounds and with no past to be raked up.

Melanie Greene matched up to the composite dream. The seventeen-year-old daughter of an international banker, she was at finishing school in Switzerland.

Elton had met her at a charity dinner attended by Prince Charles at the Ritz Hotel in 1976. Her father had been involved in the organization of the function.

The opinion of a close associate was that in the year following the *Rolling Stone* interview, Elton saw her when it suited him.

'She came to post-gig parties but was not a regular companion in the sense of being a steady girlfriend.'

From his vantage point, Andy Hill detected an omnipresent maternal guiding hand in the aftermath of Elton's published confessions.

'Whatever he may say, Elton did go through a rough time but his mother was an important ally. For his Watford duties she made it clear to him that he must maintain a proper image, attending matches in suits, et cetera. For the annual soccer presentations, he went accompanied by one of the secretaries from Rocket.

'Elton himself always kept his private life private. He was not a boastful person. Some days he would just say: "I'll be off – make your own arrangements." '

Filling the creative gap between *Blue Moves* and *A Single Man* – the first Taupin-less LP – was the second volume of greatest hits, a commendable accomplishment from an artist whose first chart entry had occurred just seven years previously.

In deference to his sporting dreams, Elton was pictured on the sleeve of the hits' compilation exhibiting readiness for a late call-up by the England cricket team. Only some natty pink trainers gave the game away.

Musically, the contents represented not merely the zenith of his commercial achievement but some of the most memorable songs he has ever recorded. 'Bennie And The Jets', 'Philadelphia Freedom', 'Sorry Seems To Be The Hardest Word', plus his joint number one with Kiki and the interpretations of 'Lucy In The Sky' and 'Pinball Wizard', which stand comparison with the exemplary originals.

Mindful of future legal acrimony, the album is also notable as the last example of a cordial professional relationship between Elton, John Reid and Dick James Music.

Both Elton and his manager shared DJM's enthusiasm for the project, down to providing the two Rocket tracks which significantly enhanced the product's marketability.

The Elton singles released during the year suffered in comparison to just about every track listed on *Greatest Hits Volume II*.

'Crazy Water' was a mundane offering from *Blue Moves* and sold as such. 'Bite Your Lip (Get Up And Dance)' was more interesting for its concept than end result. Released in Britain as a double A-side with Kiki Dee's 'Chicago', it was a rocker extended to interminable length by a succession of choruses – one critic was moved to suggest that 'Hey Jude' had a shorter denouement. The remix, by New York disco producer, Tom Moulton, illustrated Elton's willingness to explore new avenues, if predominantly to the detriment of his post 1975 releases.

Basically a shy person, Elton found solace in the company of familiar faces, professional acquaintances becoming firm friends over a passage of working time.

John Reid, Davey Johnstone, Clive Franks and Kiki Dee were among those who had stayed the course thus far. His mother remained a pivotal figure.

Moreover, certain appointments gave new meaning to the concept of the extended family. For instance, over a decade after his farewell performance at the Northwood Hills, Elton recruited the son of the landlord into his management organization.

While Elton had not maintained links with the pub in the intervening years, he did see George Hill and his family at Vicarage Road, their being avid Watford supporters.

The most enthusiastic – son Andy – was realistically contemplating life on campus when an 'out of the blue' offer from the star put his university plans on hold.

'Elton just said: "Why don't you come and work for me?" It was an opportunity I could not refuse.'

Thus, under the aegis of John Reid Enterprises, Andy became Elton's personal assistant.

The job entailed dealing with correspondence (largely lyrics speculatively submitted by aspirant songwriters), press matters and organizing part of Elton's labyrinthine itinerary, as well as ensuring a willing companion at Watford games. Elton's friends and associates were split between those whose schedules precluded attendance and the unfanatical followers, who came out of loyalty rather than desire.

As personal assistant, the teenager was also accorded privileged insight into a potentially exciting musical experiment which went sadly awry after promising beginnings.

What should have been the follow-up album to *Blue Moves* was anticipated to accrue from what became known as the Thom Bell Sessions, which took place in the autumn of 1977.

Bell was the gifted producer-arranger who completed the Philadelphia hit machine with Kenny Gamble and Leon Huff. In the manner of studio wizard, Phil Spector, a decade previously, the public would remember the songs more than the singers – although the O'Jays and Harold Melvin and the Bluenotes were two Philly acts whose fame was of some permanence.

Elton was a staunch admirer of Bell and invited him to his Los Angeles home for a conference of musical minds. Andy Hill recalled Elton asking Bell for his opinions on a chain of song ideas. Bell responded with some suggestions of his own. The sessions were a natural progression.

The famous Sigma Studios in Philly were among those used for recording and the line-up included a host of talented musicians and vocalists.

Other sessions were held in Seattle, from where Elton's party returned buoyant.

'They worked on six or seven tracks, all of them good,' Andy Hill confirmed. 'When Elton came back, he was raving about how great the album was going to be; how it was definitely going to bring him back to the top of the charts.'

The star's euphoria lasted the time it took Bell to disseminate the finished article. 'It was nothing like Elton had anticipated. He felt that too much instrumentation had been added and that it had been over-produced. He made his views known to Thom Bell, who obviously felt differently.'

The impasse put paid to an LP and it was some considerable time before a three-track single was salvaged from the creative wreckage. Even in re-mixed form, the end product justified Elton's ire at what he viewed as a missed opportunity.

However, when the disappointment of the thwarted album had abated, Elton was able to concentrate his mind on the development of the writing relationship with his new partner.

Gary Osborne was the exception which proved the rule about Elton's friendships emanating from professional liaison. Gary was a friend who happened to be around when the musical and geographical divides between Elton and Bernie were temporarily insurmountable. Though not the antithesis of Bernie Taupin, Gary was an altogether more ebullient character.

According to Andy Hill: 'Bernie was a very pleasant, very ordinary guy who could talk about anything whereas Gary was flamboyant with his wild curly blond hair and great big coats. He was not loud, but you always knew he was around.

'Elton was unhappy about his physical appearance. He would have liked to have been taller, to have longer fingers, more hair . . . I didn't appreciate it at the time, but I suppose that in some ways, he would have liked to have been Gary Osborne.'

Although Gary's own pop career had hardly made the headlines, he had done better at creating chart songs for others, a writing credit close to Elton's heart being 'Amoureuse', Kiki Dee's inaugural chart entry. But some of Gary's greatest hits had been for Lucozade, toothpaste, a bank and a building society, as he supplemented his income through the lucrative sphere of jingles for television advertisements.

Gary became an intermittent fixture at the studios where Elton was working on an album with Rocket signing, Blue. The two also regularly visited the other's home to discuss ideas. In cases of writers' block they repaired to the tennis court.

Upon his recruitment to the inner circle of Elton's staff, Andy Hill quickly discovered that he was a required addition to a list of tennis partners of unquestionable star quality. An intriguing doubles match could be made from a permutation of Elton and his sometime playing colleagues, Billie Jean King, Rod Stewart and Bryan Ferry.

While hardly possessing the physique of the natural athlete, Elton's game had benefitted immeasurably from the amalgam of professional guidance and constant practice – there were courts at both his British and American homes.

Andy Hill remembered being asked by his new boss whether he played tennis. His answer in the affirmative was challenged in their first match: 'He absolutely thrashed me.' To ensure a better level of future competition, Elton arranged tennis lessons for his personal assistant.

One of the most enjoyable of Andy Hill's early assignments in America was to accompany Elton to the Wightman Cup match, contested by the ladies of Britain and the US.

By now Elton and Billie Jean were the firmest of friends. She described him as 'a peach', he had written a song in her honour and even included her as a guest member of his band.

Therefore, Elton's awkwardness on renewing acquaintance with the

Wimbledon multi-champion seemed surprising. Andy was to learn that there were a handful of sporting and musical friends to whom Elton accorded extreme reverence.

'After a time, you get to know who he respects because he becomes very nervous in their presence. He was like that with Billie Jean.

'When he got together with Stevie Wonder after the "farewell" Wembley concert, it seemed more of an honour for Elton to meet Stevie Wonder than for Stevie Wonder to meet Elton.

'And, of course, Lennon. When we were in New York, he pointed to a window across the way from our hotel and said: "That's John Lennon's flat." He'd mention it at least once a day.'

A movie fanatic from childhood – Roy Rogers on *Goodbye Yellow Brick Road* acknowledged regular escapist hours at North Harrow ABC – it was no surprise that venerated actors and actresses comprised Elton's secondary list of the unreservedly approved. With Liz Taylor and Shirley Maclaine, the admiration was mutual, while he considered himself honoured to have had the opportunity of meeting Groucho Marx and Mae West.

As for Katharine Hepburn, she was one house guest to leave a lasting impression. On the day Hepburn cycled round to tea, a frog in the swimming pool was a particularly unwelcome sitting tenant.

Elton confessed to an irrational fear of the slimy squatter. The actress admitted to the same, yet still fished out the creature.

When questioned on how she had summoned up the courage, Hepburn replied: 'Character dear boy, character.'

Andy's character was fully tested when American commitments intruded into the British football season. Given the task of phoning home to check on how Watford fared, he would call his father at the Northwood Hills. A win would guarantee a contented employer. A defeat would presage an uncomfortable twenty-four hours: 'He was terribly passionate about the game.'

Another passion was for the resurrection of the hairline with which he had long since parted company. Though he might joke with interviewers about his decreasingly hirsute persona, it didn't amuse him anything like as much as he indicated.

As far back in his career as 'Take Me To The Pilot', Elton had expressed the, groundless, concern that the bald bassist at the session might not be able to contribute the raunchy playing essential to the track.

Indicative of Elton's vanity when his own locks deserted him was the assertion that his thinning pate was the cumulative effect of an inferior hairdressing dye – a claim conveniently failing to acknowledge that his hair was receding before the application of the putative evil lotion.

In subsequent years, the star would spend more time in hats than J. R. Ewing – many of which would have earned the approbation of the television oil baron – as successive hair transplants seemingly failed to achieve the anticipated longevity.

Eventually, Elton gained a measure of amusement from the staggering number of column inches the press devoted to his hairy escapades. In terms of his public, it was a no-loss situation. Elton's baldness had been an asset in that it further distanced him from the conventional superstar image.

Through hair transplants, he engendered sympathy and resurgent publicity at a stage when his recording and touring commitments had been wound down.

If close associates found Elton's 'vanity hair' amusing, they would wisely avoid so jesting in his presence.

Nevertheless, there were times when they were unsure whether to laugh or cry. One of Andy Hill's assignments as personal assistant was to accompany Elton for the first of a series of transplants in Paris in late 1977.

The operation was painful and intricate, involving the removal of hairs from the back of the scalp, and replanting in squares at the front.

At the completion of the surgery, Elton emerged to face the world . . . but not for very long.

Said Andy Hill: 'As he went to get into the car, he hit his head on the top of the door, knocking half the squares out. He had to return to the clinic to have them redone.'

W hether through shyness, intuition, self-preservation or John Reid's tutelage, Elton had become publicly expert at uttering a great deal while saying little. A child of the talk show generation, he had grown into the identikit guest. Give 'em a song, a few one-liners and some mildly self-deprecating jokes about clothes and hair and *voilà* – music hall for the mass media.

Occasionally, though, the mask did slip. It might be an outburst redolent of a petulant, over-indulged child. It could equally bring to mind the bravado of a naughty schoolboy no longer able to contain a guilty secret.

The former was exemplified in 1978 by a virulent attack on the British Market Research Bureau, the compiler of the most influential charts in Britain – i.e. the ones utilized by the BBC. Having remained supportively silent when his records were highly placed in the BMRB listings, he could not contain his anger the week 'Ego' dropped one place after peaking in the mid-thirties.

Having pointed out that the single was still rising (slowly) in the charts of pop papers, *Melody Maker* and *New Musical Express*, he lambasted the research bureau and allegedly threatened to withdraw Rocket advertising from publications printing the BMRB chart.

The reality of the matter was that the public didn't care for the single, which was produced by Elton and Clive Franks, bringing Gus Dudgeon's production tenancy to its conclusion – an almost simultaneous splintering to that of Elton and Bernie.

The star's version of events was that Gus Dudgeon had departed of his own volition for reasons unconnected with the music itself.

'He left the company after a board meeting, a dispute over shares, a political matter. He just got up and said: "That's it, I'm off," and walked out. But I honestly believe that after fourteen albums we needed a break from each other.'

Not only was 'Ego' the least successful British hit thus far. It did no better on the Billboard charts. Of twenty-two previous American singles, only 'Border Song' and 'Friends' fared worse in terms of chart placing.

Still acting the truculent star after his chart outburst, Elton gave a textbook example of failure to make discretion the better part of valour that same month when being interviewed by Nicky Horne on London commercial radio station, Capital.

His remark that Rocket had tried to hype a single by the group, Blue, into the charts sent shock waves through his company, with top executives denying any suggestion of sharp practice. They had to, as Elton had taken the precaution of absolving himself of responsibility during the conversation by claiming that he had no idea until after the fact that any underhand promotion had occurred.

In an interview given just before these embarrassing pronounce-ments, Elton said he tried to eschew foolhardy or immature acts. Yet 'the pampering of the pop star' rendered the irregular tantrum virtually inevitable. 'You get wrapped up in such a cocoon. You don't have to do anything for yourself. There are people to drive you anywhere, clean your shoes, plan your life. You don't have to do anything if you don't want to.'

As personal assistant, Andy Hill was privy to thunderous flashes of temper away from the public gaze. But they were literally flashes, after which equilibrium would be restored. 'Things would just build up in him until it reached the point where he would chuck a vase across the room,' Andy recalled. 'That would get it all out of his system.'

Like a bad press, for example. He took umbrage at negative coverage – particularly if it concerned his music – to the extreme of including transgressors on an unofficial blacklist.

It was not uncommon for Elton to inform a scribe from a music journal that he received bad reviews with equanimity. Minutes later, the interviewer would be treated to a barbed witticism about a writer – often from the same publication – who had written about the star's live or recorded work in less than laudatory fashion.

Conversely, Elton could also be outspoken in an altruistic sense. Again featured on Capital Radio as winner of a best singer accolade at its annual music awards, he accepted that the best man had not won.

'I don't think I deserve this. I haven't had a record out for a long time and I think this award should go to Elvis Costello.'

Anyway, he could afford to be generous, having also won the award for the best concert of 1977 (the Wembley 'farewell').

Nevertheless, the Capital honours were a shaft of light in what, from a professional standpoint, had been a fairly miserable start to 1978.

The rumour was that Bernie had submitted half-a-dozen sets of lyrics for the next album, all of which had been rejected by Elton. Andy Hill got the impression that Bernie favoured a disco-oriented LP, which Elton didn't consider a viable project.

'Simply, they were going through a difficult patch. It wasn't personal. It wasn't really about where Bernie lived. It was musical – they were progressing in very different ways.'

Kiki Dee considered a temporary dissolution an inevitability after a decade spent in a high pressure working environment. 'It was a communication problem. An unbelievable amount had happened to them over a ten-year period and they just needed some time apart.'

For the benefit of the press, Elton went through the platitudes such situations necessitate. He and Bernie were good friends and would, doubtless, collaborate again before too long.

Another rumour more difficult to quash concerned Elton's displeasure at the way Rocket was headed. Since 1973, only he, Kiki and Blue had enjoyed hits on the label in Britain (Neil Sedaka had proved a shrewd Stateside acquisition).

Later in the year, it was announced that Rocket had severed its connections with EMI and that a distribution deal had been agreed with Phonogram.

Kiki herself was departing, although on amicable terms. 'I think it was mutually accepted that I should go,' she explained. 'I felt a bit stagnant and in need of a change.

'A lot of people had high aspirations of me and I felt I had to get away to work out what I really wanted for myself.'

Interestingly, Kiki's considered judgement was that Elton and John Reid had lost their initial zest for the project. 'No one was really at the centre of things,' she commented, adding the boxing analogy: 'Maybe it wasn't a hungry label.'

Hungry or otherwise, there was no lack of innovation in support of Elton's vinyl offerings.

In the days before the video promotional film for a new single was commonplace, a reported £50,000 had been spent on a promo short for 'Ego' which enjoyed press showings in Britain and America.

'I feel the only way I can communicate at the moment is through movies,' was Elton's explanation of sorts. The more cynical among the film's media audience suggested that the film was the only way of communicating sympathetically the limited impact of his first transplant surgery. Far less was made of the film than the fact that Elton arrived for the Los Angeles première with a baseball cap covering the famous scalp. In all probability, the ludicrous concentration on what might or might not be under his headgear contributed to Elton's surly countenance when the press switched the focus to other matters.

Responding to a question about the live capabilities of some of the top-line rock acts, he was particularly scathing. Would he be going to watch David Bowie in concert in Los Angeles? 'I wouldn't cross the road to see him.' And so on.

Ironically, Elton's rantings remained consistent with the sort of music industry excess the single was meant to highlight.

'I made a statement in "Ego",' he subsequently commented. 'It was about the type of people you can meet in this business, with over-inflated ideas and big talk. They're the types I loathe.'

In Britain, meanwhile, the great hair debate continued *ad nauseam* in the national press. One paper used a clip from the film depicting Elton with a 'luxuriant' growth of hair. The riposte of a rival journal was to claim that the picture was in soft focus and had been touched up anyway.

It was hard not to sympathize with his irritation as he pointed out that Bob Dylan's appearance at Blackbushe before a record audience was hidden away inside the pages of *The Sun* on the same day that the tabloid had splashed a picture of a hat-less Elton on its front cover.

At a crossroads in his personal and professional life, Elton's haven from home was his soccer club, and the game in general.

Leaving for Hawaii in June, Elton told reporters that his exodus was timed to avoid television coverage of the World Cup. 'Like a lot of people, I've had enough of football on the box,' he declared.

Yet he was soon back in Britain for a fund-raising event benefitting his pet sporting charity, Goaldiggers – and displaying a broad hint that his retirement from concerts was nearing an end.

At the function, held at London's Dorchester Hotel, Elton had been quite easily coerced into playing two songs for 'auction' bids. After intimating that he would be previewing something new, he mischievously launched into to 'Candle In The Wind', followed by 'Your Song'. However, instead of then vacating the stage, he went on to perform an extended set.

By the football season 1978–79, match days at Vicarage Road had become a veritable pleasure as Watford continued on a winning path. Away excursions were equally gratifying, although Elton had cause to rue his choice from an extravagant motoring selection when Watford opened their third division campaign with a single-goal victory at Walsall.

His car broke down on the M1, forcing him to return home in ignominy to await news of the scoreline.

A more fulfilling travelling experience saw the team recall past giant-killing feats by defeating the mighty Manchester United at their own Old Trafford ground in a League Cup match. For an emotional chairman, the victory represented 'the greatest moment of my life in football,' a sentiment he was to continually re-apply as success bred success.

No one gained greater pleasure from Elton's involvement at Watford than his mother. 'Watford has brought him down to earth again,' opined Sheila Farebrother. 'He's mixing with ordinary people. He's never been more happy.

'You don't find real, true friends in the entertainment world. They all want to climb up the ladder. They all want to use you. I think Elton knows that.'

Elton seemingly did, agreeing that the football fraternity were more straightforward than their showbiz counterparts. 'In rock 'n' roll, you never really know who's on your side.'

In November 1978, Watford's progress should have been the least of Elton's worries as he was rushed to a top London clinic with chest pains. Heart trouble was a worrying possibility, but the eventual diagnosis was that the condition was the product of an exhausting life.

The patient's recipe for 'the perfect get well card?' To arrange for a telephone line to be kept open to the press box at Exeter FC, where Watford were playing. The bedside supporter was rewarded with a 2–0 win.

But the public levity masked private concern. An earlier collapse on the tennis court had been kept from the media. Elton unwisely came up with the self-prognosis of a condition curable by a few days rest. It might even have sufficed had he then not relaunched himself into a schedule of play as debilitating as a rigorous working programme.

The run-up to the more serious attack went as follows: A week of heavy television and press commitments. Then, having played football on Sunday at a five-a-side event at Wembley, Elton reportedly spent a gruelling three hours on the tennis court the following day with Billie Jean King. It was on Tuesday that he keeled over at home after making a telephone call. 'I had terrible pains in my chest, arms and legs,' he recalled. 'I couldn't breathe – I could hardly move for the pain.'

Summoning help via an aide, he was rushed to the Harley Street Clinic, where he was detained for three days.

'This has really shaken me,' he admitted. 'When you are used to non-stop tours across the States and so on, you start to think you are super human. Then something like this happens and you realize you're not. Sometimes, you've got to slow down like everyone else.'

During this period of revision, Elton had time to contemplate the contradictions of his life. He was fabulously wealthy – 'I handed the taxman a cheque for £1,800,000 last year, but I'm not complaining.' He had been phenomenally successful – the top-selling recording artist of the early and mid–1970s. Yet after almost a decade of achievement, he literally couldn't cross a road on his own. 'It reached the point where I was helpless.' Not that he was a rock 'n' roll casualty – on the contrary, friends acknowledged a shrewd business brain supplementing his musical gifts. He had just lost the habit of taking care of everyday niceties himself.

Thankfully, the prerequisites of his football chairmanship had injected a dose of reality into a life hitherto dominated by the ersatz universe of the music business.

It was down to him to plead Watford's case before the bank manager. Or to try and arrange accommodation for the players. For too long, such responsibilities in his own life had been assigned to others.

A year previously, Elton had acted the prima donna when an error by TWA resulted in there being no seat for him on a transatlantic flight. (In fairness to the airline, the then predilection for making bookings for the star in names connected with hair must have been confusing.)

Now he could recount with childlike pride: 'I got really excited the other day when I went abroad. I booked my own flight, got the plane on my own and checked into a hotel all by myself. A few years ago, I would have had it all done for me. I thought, "here you are at the age of thirty-one and, at last, you can do it on your own".'

This new self-assurance coincided with the release of A *Single Man*. The first original LP for two years it, as promised, heralded a new, if hardly glittering era.

Clive Franks, who added bass guitar to his producer's credits, was the sole survivor from the earliest days. The new boys were Tim

Renwick on guitar and Steve Holly, who maintained the tradition of drummers poached from Kiki Dee's band.

From a sales standpoint, the album justified the 'Ego' sessions. For having gone into the studios solely to work on the single after a period of comparative inactivity, his mood was conducive to more substantial accomplishment.

Explained Clive Franks: 'He was tinkling away on the piano between takes, and by the time we had finished the single, he had ideas for six songs.' The LP took off from there.

When Elton later suggested the producer doubling up on bass for the album sessions, Clive construed the offer as either a joke or a capricious gesture to be quickly forgotten. After all, Clive's tenure as a band member was no more than a professional interlude in an obscure outfit called Fables at the tail end of the 1960s.

He only accepted the appointment as gospel when no other bassist arrived to start the recordings.

Understandably self-conscious about his dual role, Clive's early reaction was that the job combination was not a propitious one. 'But Elton gave me confidence – and when I listened to the finished product, there were times when I smiled to myself and thought: "That's me".'

After the exotic locations of past recordings, it was off to deepest Berkshire for A *Single Man*, very handy indeed for Watford home games. Taking advantage of the close proximity, Elton fulfilled a cherished goal – to work in the studios with the players on material superior to the truly appalling footballing songs that manifest annually around cup final time.

On that score, the participation of the Watford squad on two tracks – 'Big Dipper' and 'Georgia' – was no great surprise. What did dumbfound Clive Franks was the professionalism displayed by the footballers in unfamiliar surroundings. 'Twenty-five players were at the session, including one or two excellent singers. There was only one atrocious voice, but he was kept well away from a mike – anyway, one out of twenty-five isn't bad.'

Keith Mercer, one of the footballing chorus line, found the experience reminiscent of an important away fixture. 'We all travelled together to the studios on a coach one evening. 'Big Dipper' I think we got on the first or second take. For 'Georgia' . . . well, that took a bit of doing.

'The players had a great time. We had a few beers – in fact, it wasn't until we started drinking that we got the songs right.'

The vast majority of the tracks were John–Osborne credits. The remainder were by Elton alone. Of his former writing partner, he commented: 'He might get dreadfully upset because there's not one track of his on the album. But it'll give him a much needed kick up the arse.'

Replacing Bernie Taupin, Gary Osborne accepted that he was on a hiding to nothing. 'I know I won't get the credit if the album is a success. I will only get the blame if it fails.

'I have the highest admiration for Bernie's work. He would write the lyrics, hand them over and Elton would have to set them to music. We do it the other way round – Elton is the instigator now.

'He seems to have found a whole new stock of melodies. My job is to put words to them.'

Not surprisingly for one fresh from working on commercials, Gary expressed his contribution to A *Single Man* as being his most satisfying ever. 'I don't consider it to be a one-off job. I hope we'll continue writing together.' By the same token, the album's lightweight lyrical content can hardly have been unforeseen from a writer newly unleashed from extolling the virtues of the paste which leaves teeth sparkling.

Commercially, nevertheless, the first single from the album, 'Part-Time Love', was a significant improvement on 'Ego'. If breaking no new musical ground, it had the virtue of simplicity, showcasing one of those trademark melodies that Elton is probably capable of composing in his sleep.

The artist was content to concur all the way to the bank. 'The album is a very sensitive one [and] simpler than the stuff I've done before, reflecting the time that I took to take stock of my situation.'

As if anticipating a rough reception for Gary Osborne's first set of lyrics, he added: 'I don't think that politics in music ever have much of an effect. Look at all the singers in the sixties who tried to change the world through words. Life continued much the same.'

Buyers in Britain and America made 'Part-Time Love' his highest placed single on both sides of the Atlantic since 'Sorry Seems To Be The Hardest Word'.

By now, Elton's records had to compete for attention with the more pithy sentiments of the first wave of established punk bands.

Admitting that an early television sighting of the Sex Pistols had made him feel of pensionable age, he had no hesitation in expressing admiration for many of the bands – even though none were willing to jeopardize their street credibility through reciprocal approbation.

In the era of the sartorial safety pin, platform shoes and glittering outfits were but a tame memory. Nevertheless, Elton made the comparison for the benefit of readers of *New Musical Express*.

'Everything I do is very tongue-in-cheek. That's why I enjoy the punk thing. I look at 'em and think: "What a fucking state they're in," then remember that when I first went to Watford, I was six foot three and had pink hair. Now I'm five foot eight and have hardly any hair at all. I even used to dye my eyebrows pink. And those stupid shoes. . .'

The irascible demeanour of earlier in the year had been supplanted by a new enthusiasm.

A month had passed since Elton had professed to contentment away from the concert arena in the year since the dramatic announcement at Wembley. 'I'd lost my hunger to perform. I'd done everything, playing in small halls and huge stadia. There didn't seem to be anything left.'

Now came the about-face. Barely an eyebrow was raised when the world was informed that Elton would be back on stage early in the new year. Both management and record label declined to elaborate on the reasoning behind the policy reversal. But it was safe to assume that, leaving aside his penchant for the dramatic, the Barnum in Elton once more craved an audience beyond recording studio personnel and talk-show ticket-holders.

With only Ray Cooper for stage company and the venues on the smallish side, the proposed itinerary stayed true to a past intention to eschew the grandiose setting . . . like Central Park, New York, where eighteen months later, Elton played before a cosy 400,000–plus attendance.

The tour dates – announced in January 1979 – covered Sweden, Germany, Holland and France. The focal point of the British segment was a residency at the Theatre Royal Drury Lane.

Meanwhile, another track from *A Single Man* had gone on to provide Elton with a first instrumental hit.

'Song For Guy' was a haunting memorial to Guy Burchett, a seventeen-year-old messenger boy at Rocket Records, who was killed in a motorcycle accident. As a reminder of the old days, a previously unreleased John–Taupin composition, 'Lovesick', was nominated as the B-side.

Rising to number four, 'Song For Guy' was also notable as Elton's first self-penned top ten single in Britain since 1973. In addition, it won him an Ivor Novello award.

As a counterpoint to A *Single Man*, DJM released a series of double A-sided singles in an unashamed attempt to generate further capital from the star's back catalogue, sales having been dormant since the release of the second volume of greatest hits.

Ethical considerations aside – and DJM would contend that ethics were a two-way street – the coupling of, say, 'Goodbye Yellow Brick Road' and 'Sweet Painted Lady' (or 'Your Song' and 'Border Song') wiped the floor with the current material.

Having seen in 1979 at a party at Mayfair nightclub, Maunkberrys, in the company of Rod Stewart and Rolling Stones, Ronnie Wood and Keith Richards, Elton readied himself for his stage return.

Sensibly scheduled to begin outside Britain, Elton found himself 'shaking and bloody lonely' before facing an audience in Stockholm in February. 'It was a good start and it's going to get better,' was the performer's post-gig verdict.

In Paris – a regular commuting point as his hair treatment progressed – Elton took particular pleasure in earning the plaudits of all in the Champs-Elysées Theatre. France had been the hardest commercial territory to conquer – in fact, appearing at the same venue early in his career, he was reportedly pelted with rotten fruit.

There was no danger of audience displeasure when Elton returned to the London stage, Drury Lane patrons being treated to a three-hour set. He was in similarly bubbly form at a party in his honour at London nightspot, Legends.

In keeping with the venue's title, invitees were instructed to attend disguised as a legendary figure.

Among a guest list encompassing Marlene Dietrich, Rudolph Valentino, Ginger Rogers and Robin Hood, Elton ensured the limelight by turning up sporting a blond curly wig and claiming to be Rod Stewart.

Ignoring the odd petulant interlude, the strong friendship between two of the most charismatic characters in rock had continued unabated.

Supplementing the Baldry connection, they adored football, played tennis to win and frequented each other's haunts. When, invoking nostalgia, Elton returned to the Northwood Hills, he was treated very much as a regular, the novelty of young Reggie Dwight making good having withered with time. On a solitary visit, Stewart caused more of a stir at the hostelry than Elton ever did.

Rod called Elton 'Sharon'. Elton christened Rod 'Phyllis', and was not a million miles from the scene of the crime when a banner was rigged up outside London's Olympia, where Stewart was performing during the festive season. It read: 'Blondes have more fun but brunettes have lots more money. Happy Christmas Phyllis. Love Sharon.'

The banner was hastily removed.

Rod was the intended co-star in a doomed film project conceived late the previous year.

Missing out on *Harold and Maude* – 'one of the greatest movies of all time and the best script' – had been the exception which proved the rule of Elton's credo for achievement: 'Being in the right place at the right time.'

The star had continued to rue his lost opportunity in the intervening years. All he had to show as a performing credit was his cameo as the Pinball Wizard in *Tommy*. Yet in the approaching 1980s, even that could be written off as a nice promo for a single.

Scriptwise, it had then been 'downhill all the way'. Maybe *Jet Lag* would only have continued the slide.

Jet Lag was the working title for the projected cinematic collaboration, to be produced by the stars' respective managers, John Reid and Billy Gaff.

The idea was for Rod and Elton to portray characters similar to themselves. The pre-promotion predicted a comedy redolent of the 'Road' films immortalized by Bob Hope and Bing Crosby.

Elton commented at the inception: 'It will be a film about the rock business that leans towards the funny side of it and some of the incredible things which go on.

'My idea for the opening is to have two superstars landing in their private jets in LA and jamming up the runway because neither of them wants to get out first. I could name two or three people who would do that.'

Originally, the movie was intended to go into production in the latter half of 1979. Under the proffered excuse of conflicting commitments, the project was put on an interminable hold until it was finally abandoned two years later.

News from the football front was infinitely more palatable. With or without their chairman's presence, the Watford players kept on winning to clinch promotion for the second successive year.

In another impeccably timed strike, the crucial points were collected in a match against Hull City, just as Elton was due to chart new and prestigious touring territory . . . Russia.

'I'm drinking lemonade now, but I'm going to have a good night and a hangover in the morning,' declared the upwardly mobile chairman. In an apposite parting gesture, Elton presented the Watford manager, Graham Taylor, with a gold disc for sales of A *Single Man*.

The invitation for Elton to give concerts in the Soviet Union could be construed as something of a loaded compliment. In essence, it suggested that, having vetted his material and stage show, the authorities considered Elton an agent unlikely to subvert the minds of Russian youth.

It also represented an incalculable publicity coup in the year preceding an Olympics controversially awarded to Moscow.

For an artist professedly concerned with reaching as many confirmed or potential fans as possible, any political considerations were not of great import. Elton had made plain his stance on such issues when returning recently from a series of concerts in Israel. Acknowledging that the dates would probably preclude invitations from Arab countries, he stated that politics had no part in music.

So off he went to the Soviet Union in May, unprepared totally for the warmth of both climate and reception.

A Soviet journal summarized the appeal of the VIP visitor with the immortal sentence: 'Audiences are specially attracted to the lyrical ballads and folk songs performed by R. Dwight.' But the loyal coterie of fans who somehow managed to lay hands on the small percentage of concert tickets made available to the general public exhibited no such ignorance.

Those less fortunate were prepared to pay prices excessive even by black market standards to see the concerts in Moscow and Leningrad. Tickets priced £5 were reputedly changing hands for twenty times that amount.

The first Leningrad performance at the Oktyabrsky Hall presented a new dilemma for Soviet police and officials – how to respond to audience members dancing in the aisles. Spurred by the fans' reaction, 'R. Dwight' decided to end the show with a stirring rendition of 'Back In The USSR'.

Further unprecedented problems were caused to the law enforcers outside the venue as thousands of young people spilled over barriers and a police chain to catch a final glimpse of the singer, who reciprocated by waving from his dressing room window.

Pleased at how the concerts had been received and touched at the lengths to which Soviet fans had gone to obtain his records, an elated Elton described the tour as the fulfilment of another challenge.

'It was marvellous. I felt like Bob Dylan. The last show in Moscow was probably one of the best concerts I've given in my life, simply because the kids inspired me.'

Recalling the 'incredible friendliness' of the young Russians who had chanted his name in the street outside the Leningrad concert hall, Elton added: 'We've been invited to return and we will definitely be going, although I don't know when.'

More seriously, he was conscious of the need for fresh incentives, having achieved so prodigiously in commercial terms.

'One of the reasons I wanted to go [to Russia] is that I didn't know what to expect. That makes you play harder.'

'I wanted to get back my self-respect and start enjoying life again. I could not keep on playing in Britain and the US. It is safe, but it drains you.'

British fans were given a taste of the historic shows through a short film, *To Russia With Elton*, which played as a support feature in cinemas.

The men behind the project were Dick Clement and Ian La Frenais – writers with a successful background in comedy – who travelled around with the touring party.

Triumphant on his return, Elton threw himself into the sort of maniacal schedule which had contributed to past physical problems.

There were further rewarding days – for example, a visit to the Royal School for the Deaf in Derby, where he met pupils: 'They can't hear the music but enjoy the vibration,' he said by way of explanation of a performance there. But it was primarily work. A 'holiday' in the South of France was utilized to work on a forthcoming album, *21 At 33*, at the Superbear Studios in Nice.

Although Elton's rented house was only a matter of miles from the studios, negotiating the winding roads between the two properties was a lengthy affair. In consequence, the star could often be found sleeping on the studio floor.

In contrast to his writing partner, he just could not relax. Gary Osborne admitted that while he could happily lie in the sun all day,

Elton 'would go for a swim, then play croquet, then play piano, then sit in the sun. He can't take it easy. He finds it very hard to relax.'

Still, Elton exuded contentment before jetting off for his first American tour since 1976, audaciously themed 'Back In The USSA', in recognition of his contribution to musical detente in the Soviet Union.

Press at the airport were even treated to a progress check on his hair transplants, for which he said there were two treatments outstanding.

Again travelling light with only Ray Cooper for musical company, the intention was similarly to perform in small and medium-sized auditoriums, as opposed to the stadia gigs of past and future.

What Elton could not escape was the universal antipathy towards *Victim Of Love*, an album inviting one of two interpretations. The first: A brave but flawed attempt to take a new musical direction. The second: An unmitigated disaster.

Elton's love of blues and soul was unquestioned. He was totally sincere when once commenting: 'I'm such a black record fanatic. To think that I'm actually in the R. & B. chart means that even if it doesn't get any higher than thirty-four [his record's position that week], I'm gonna stick it up and frame it.'

With the avowed intention of experimenting musically, he had been receptive to an approach for collaboration on a disco album by Pete Bellotte, whose reputation was largely built working with studio wizard, Giorgio Moroder, and Donna Summer, mistress of the seductive single.

As a possible foretaste of what was to come, Rocket had finally released a maxi-single at the start of the year from the Thom Bell Sessions in 1977 which, in Elton's eyes, had initially promised so much.

Even remixed in London by Elton and Clive Franks, 'Are You Ready For Love?' 'Three Way Love Affair' and 'Mama Can't Buy You Love', all justified Elton's qualms about Bell's emphasis on production values over substance.

With 'Are You Ready For Love?' as the A-side, the single peaked outside the British top forty. Nevertheless, the Stateside audience had proved more appreciative. MCA had led with 'Mama Can't Buy You Love' and were rewarded with a top ten record.

In his heart of hearts, Elton realized that *Victim Of Love* would do little for his credibility.

Rumours emanating from the Musicland Studios in Munich suggested that fans should prepare themselves for something different. What was not explained was that for 'different', they should transpose 'regressive'.

Interviewed at the time of its release, Elton seemed eager to put as much distance as possible between himself and the product under discussion.

'It all started when Pete Bellotte asked if I'd like to do a disco album with him. I can't write that kind of music so he wrote the words and music. I only sang the songs. The keyboard parts are played by two other musicians. I know I'm going to get knocked for the album.' The thesis was correct.

Elton's partnership with Pete Bellotte can be comfortably be nominated as the least fruitful of his career. In the context of *Victim Of Love*, the belated release from the Thom Bell liaison comes across as innovative.

Some idea of the disparate forces at work can be gleaned from the bizarre inclusion of a cover version of the Chuck Berry classic, 'Johnny B Goode'.

The title track from *Victim Of Love* fared poorly in the singles market on both sides of the Atlantic. Even the reappearance of Elton as a touring attraction failed to lift it into the American top thirty.

Whatever his US fans thought of the new album, it was business as usual for the concert dates. The fans loved the two-man shows. The critics were divided.

Reviewing the first of a week of October concerts at the Palladium, New York, the critic from the *New York Times*, Robert Palmer, considered the performance in terms of a 'supper club ambience ... He's just about ready for Las Vegas.' While Palmer acknowledged that the audience didn't share his viewpoint, there remained the school of thought that, pared to the instrumental bone, Elton's songs translated as lightweight.

By now, Elton had become as accustomed to criticism from the New York media as he was of remaining in the headlines of the British press. While in foreign lands, his name was featured prominently in coverage of a High Court action brought by the former England soccer boss, Don Revie, against his erstwhile employers, the Football Association.

Revie had told the court that the FA officials had been moved to apoplexy at the cost of a champagne party enjoyed by the England players after a victory in Helsinki – that is, until Elton stepped in and offered to pay.

Critics notwithstanding, Elton was pleased with the reaction to the solo gigs in America. 'Returning to America has been the most important thing,' he declared. 'I have my enthusiasm for concerts back and am already thinking about putting a band together next year.'

He was also more confident about other aspects of life. 'The big glasses and the weird clothes were a way of hiding my shyness. Since I started wearing contact lenses I've had to overcome that. I was forced to look people in the face and you have to find confidence from somewhere to do that.'

While perceiving a change in her son, Sheila Farebrother was moved to describe him as 'a Jekyll and Hyde character. Off stage, he's rather less self-confident. He is still Reg Dwight at times. Shy, he withdraws from people.

'Deep down, he thinks – or used to at any rate – that he's the ugliest thing that ever walked. That's why he hid behind his 179 pairs of glasses for so long.'

16

The album title *21 At 33* said it all. The 21 represented the number of LPs recorded. The 33 denoted the age of the artist, a handy juncture to restore credibility before the onset of rock 'n' roll dotage.

After the shambles of *Victim Of Love*, the new album earned a respectable reception, having benefitted from Elton's judicious pairing with writing partners old, recent and new.

'Little Jeannie' – his best received American single since 'Island Girl' – could have been a throwback to the vintage John–Taupin repertoire, whereas it was written with Gary Osborne.

Bernie Taupin was back among the fold, contributing to three tracks, while the stylish 'Sartorial Eloquence' was the most effective of the two songs written in harness with Tom Robinson – one of the more substantial talents to have emerged from the new wave, not least for being unafraid to focus on homosexual issues.

The final track, 'Give Me The Love', was co-authored by Judie Tzuke, Rocket's latest – and as it transpired last-bid to find a stellar alternative to their major asset. A six-figure sum had been invested in the delicate songstress, the most tangible early return being a top twenty single, 'Stay With Me Till Dawn'.

Primarily recorded during Elton's putative holiday in Nice the previous summer, *21 At 33* also saw Clive Franks recalled to co-production duty.

However, possibly the album's greatest significance concerned the personnel on the side two opener, 'White Lady, White Powder', which was added in Los Angeles in the early part of 1980. The participation in the latter sessions of Dee Murray and Nigel Olsson suggested an impending return from the wilderness. Under the circumstances, it seems almost superfluous to mention that Don Henley and Glenn Frey of erstwhile concert support, the Eagles, added lustre to the chorus.

If *21 At 33* offered an indication of a return to the original formation, the *rapprochement* was cemented during another American tour in 1980.

With Dee and Nigel joining Davey Johnstone, James Newton Howard and guitarists Richie Zito and Tim Renwick, the band was up to the requisite strength for a concert landmark the equal of Moscow and Leningrad.

Before the largest audience of his concert life, Elton gave a free show in Central Park. The concert – ostensibly organized to promote the city's need to preserve its parks and open spaces – will best be remembered for a reinvigorated Elton stomping through the high-spots of those twenty-one LPs.

Fans in the best vantage points were amply rewarded for their two-day vigil by a close-up of the clothing variations of the resplendent star.

Quite apart from the infamous duck costume, which took weeks of construction work, Elton's sartorial splendour for the delectation of the masses ran to a fetching sequinned Western outfit and a racy little keyboard number.

Despite the departure from the one-man show format, many of the most sensitive songs were showcased – 'Little Jeannie', 'Goodbye Yellow Brick Road', 'Sorry Seems To Be The Hardest Word' and 'Someone Saved My Life Tonight'.

There were also inclusions of especial relevance to the artist – 'the song I wrote for Miss Billie Jean King' ('Philadelphia Freedom') and 'a song written by a friend of mine' ('Imagine').

Augmented by such traditional concert staples as 'Bennie And The Jets', 'Saturday Night's Alright (For Fighting)' and, of course, 'Your Song', the performance had covered the consummate Elton collection.

The star would later declare that a Watford appearance in a Wembley cup final outstripped the Central Park experience. But it had provided a mighty tough act to follow.

While the numerically titled album was the only collection of original material released during 1980, competition was provided from the source of another re-issue package from Elton's former company.

Lady Samantha served as a valuable curio compilation for neophytes labouring under the misapprehension that Elton's formative work began with the recording of 'Your Song'.

Aside from the title track (the first single to attract any kind of recognition), the LP afforded a pot-pourri of early exploration. There was the re-recorded version of 'Skyline Pigeon' which appeared as the flip of the 'Daniel' single, the theme song and 'The Honey Roll' from the unloved soundtrack album, *Friends*, and a disparate selection of B-sides.

'Grey Seal' had initially accompanied 'Rock And Roll Madonna' in 1970 before a revised version was included on the *Goodbye Yellow Brick Road* LP in 1973. 'Rock And Roll Madonna' (also featured) itself became a B-side when DJM released 'Bennie And The Jets' in 1976 in the vain hope of a repetition of its earlier American sales.

Then there is 'Ho Ho Ho (Who'd Be A Turkey At Christmas?)', the sparring partner to the minor festive hit, 'Step Into Christmas'. The sort of discursive singalong ditty which would have boosted the collection in the days of Reggie Dwight, pub pianist, it introduced Watford Football Club into his music by way of some banal lyrics.

If it seemed inexplicable that the record was now being put out, six years after the release of a cassette compilation of the same material, DJM could cite renewed interest in the artist. Having declined to raid the vaults at the time of Elton's departure, the company had belatedly plumped for the closest option.

Meanwhile, Elton was still assiduously discharging his football duties. He commuted 12,000 miles to witness a goalless draw between his club and Charlton, only to have his frustration heightened by the disclosure that the local council had rejected a multi-million pound development plan which would have given Watford a stadium second to none in the English game.

In a fit of pique, he announced to the press: 'I am absolutely furious and will consider taking the club to a neighbouring borough.'

Back in Los Angeles to record, he took time off for another telephone link-up with Watford's local hospital broadcasting service for the team's FA Cup-tie against Arsenal.

'I would love to be there, but at the moment I have these few albums to finish,' was the blasé explanation. 'Every now and then I have to put my career first and Watford second.'

A great advocate of the hospital radio coverage, he said the live commentary it provided was infinitely preferable to regular telephone checks with the club. Even if things were going awry on the pitch, it was better to have a continuous damage assessment.

Increasingly closeted in faraway lands, Elton's chairmanship was largely conducted by phone as Watford started fulfilling the expectations of his childhood dreams.

He was listening in anxiously from Phoenix, Arizona, when Watford scored a notable triumph over the European champions, Nottingham Forest. With Christmas beckoning, he was on the line from Australia for ball-by-ball commentaries.

'Because of the amount of touring I did last year, I must be the only football chairman who never saw his team win last season.'

Yet once more revising his retirement age – 'I don't want to go on touring when I'm thirty-seven or thirty-eight –' Elton's present justification for his punitive schedule was to assure his financial future.

On his opulent uppers, he exercised selective amnesia over past mishaps as a consequence of compulsive overwork – the 1978 collapse, a 'flu bug' which caused him to keel over on stage in Los Angeles and a parlous state of health which necessitated wheelchair transportation through Sydney Airport.

Dick James could not dissuade Elton from excessive industry in the early days. For all his influence in other spheres, John Reid was no more persuasive in getting his charge to relax in latter years – at least, in the truest sense of the word.

Explained Kiki Dee: 'Elton and John Reid are a great combination as manager and artist. You only have to look at how long they've been together. But while Elton may be content to let John guide him in business matters, he is not the type to say "yes sir, no sir" if he disagrees. On creative issues he always calls the shots.'

One of Elton's less arduous assignments in the coming months was to record a follow-up duet with Kiki to 'Don't Go Breaking My Heart', five years after the worldwide number one.

Now clear of Rocket's orbit, Kiki had decided to record the Tamla classic, 'Loving You Is Sweeter Than Ever', for her forthcoming Ariola LP, *Perfect Timing*.

She had already completed the vocals when she played the track to Elton one evening. Never equivocal about anything Motown, he loved the song, Kiki's interpretation, and offered his presence at the studio to add a vocal track.

Another duet unreleased in Britain had given Elton a number one in France, where he was encamped for the spring. 'Les Aveux' – recorded with native songstress, France Gall – made him top of the pops in a country where recognition had come tardily.

During the year, Elton's view of Britain was largely confined to the picturesque environment of the transfer lounge at Heathrow Airport. In April he was passing through from Paris *en route* to Los Angeles to shoot a promotional film for the year's album, *The Fox*. Back again from Paris in November, the star decreed Britain too cold to endure and jetted back out in the direction of the Caribbean. The alternative enticement of a Watford fixture at Bolton proved no contest.

The Fox was significant for two reasons. The first album for his new American label, Geffen, it also introduced Chris Thomas as producer.

All the signs were that, as with DJM in 1976, Elton's departure from MCA was not without rancour. The catalyst was 'Song For Guy', so well received by the British public and reviewers but a Stateside débâcle.

The reason cited by MCA for the track's unsuitability as an American single was that another instrumental – 'Music Box Dancer' by Frank Mills – was already in the Billboard listings. Apparently, the wisdom concerning instrumentals was that one was sufficient to flood the market.

It piqued Elton to see a single of which he was justifiably proud released without promotion in the world's top selling place. Resultantly, it failed to reach the hot 100.

Likewise, once positively gleeful about possessing an eight million dollar asset, corporate statements from MCA had latterly dealt primarily with austerity measures. Whereas a few years back the company had thrown a party in honour of their star attraction with an intimate guest list of 800, president, Robert Siner, commented that the way forward was to have a list of three – ' and they have to bring their own lunch'.

If Elton was to switch allegiance, what better to contemplate than the label which issued John Lennon's final records? And if considering an alteration in production, who better to engage than a man whose credits had run the gamut from Roxy Music to the Sex Pistols?

The Fox was not a fair product on which to judge Thomas as half the tracks remained under the production aegis of Elton and Clive Franks.

Geffen's reward was two hits of medium proportion, the best of which, 'Nobody Wins', made it to the fringe of the American top twenty.

Elton's only major British date of the year was by royal command. In 1972 he had been irked – putting it mildly – to have interrupted an American tour to take his place in the line-up at the Royal Variety Show.

Now it was a cause for pride that he had been requested to play at Prince Andrew's twenty-first birthday party at Windsor Castle.

Where Princess Margaret had led the way, the younger royal

generation had followed. When Prince Andrew married Sarah Ferguson – a wedding attracting only marginally more media attention than Elton's own – the star and his wife were on the guest list.

At the peak of his popularity in 1974, Elton John had welcomed a very special guest on stage at his Thanksgiving concert at Madison Square Garden, New York, whose appearance was the corollary to a lighthearted studio wager.

When Elton had played keyboards on John Lennon's 'Whatever Gets You Through The Night', he had suggested that should the record make number one in America, the former Beatle would owe him a concert guest spot.

When the single reached the top slot, Lennon kept his word, giving the MSG audience a cameo to remember, duetting with Elton on the single, 'Lucy In The Sky' and 'I Saw Her Standing There'.

A godfather to Sean, Lennon's son by Yoko Ono, Elton was devastated when Lennon was killed by an assassin's bullet in 1980.

Two years later a tribute to him, 'Empty Garden (Hey Hey Johnny)', was included on the *Jump Up* album and also released as a single. It will hardly be remembered as one of his biggest sellers, peaking outside the British top fifty and making number 13 in the States. But it was a irrefutably poignant moment for Elton when Yoko and Sean Lennon came to Madison Square Garden to publicly thank him for the tribute.

Elton had returned to MSG, a habitual stamping ground, for a series of concerts as vibrant as any which had preceded them down the years. Furthermore, he was back in harness with the original Elton John band members, Olsson, Murray and Johnstone.

New York was certainly his kind of town when it boasted the type of video outlet facilitating volume purchase in the manner of his beloved Tower Records. Employees of one such establishment equated Elton with a small boy in a toy shop as he purchased 150 pre-recorded tapes in one brief spree.

Visually, the highlight of Elton's stage attire this trip was conservative by the benchmark of past visits. Bereft of inspiration as to a method of safely spiriting the star before a massive open-air audience in St Louis, the local constabulary hit upon the idea of disguising him as a policeman.

Even in the requisite uniform, the concept was doomed to failure. Cries of 'look there's Elton' were supplanted by shouts of 'look there's Elton dressed as a policeman'. Still, the jacket, pants and gun holster were among Elton's luggage when he flew back to Heathrow after the ten-week tour. And the regulation issue cap? He was wearing it.

For the moment, the positive side of his character was in clear ascendency, with events on the football field decisively contributing.

When Elton had assumed the Watford chairmanship in 1976, the popular view was of a homely club likely to oscillate between the lower divisions. The periodic boost of a cup giant-killing would be insufficient to sustain the star's interest after a couple of indifferent league campaigns.

As invariably the case, Elton was to have the last laugh over his detractors. Amidst his world travels he maintained daily contact with the club, even shelling out a thousand pounds to receive live commentary on four crucial fixtures – all won. 'It was worth every penny,' he commented. 'I couldn't bear to be out of touch.'

Elton was on tour in Norway in May when Watford earned their place among the footballing aristocracy, a 2–0 victory over Wrexham guaranteeing a first division berth. Although quoted as saying that money would be no object in ensuring that he was in attendance when his team qualified for the premier league, contractual obligations mitigated against this.

However, hastening an Oslo concert to a slightly premature conclusion, he caught the last minutes of the match on a phone link to a hospital radio service.

'I wish I was there to see the fans going bananas,' he told reporters. For their part, the Vicarage Road faithful would have welcomed the opportunity to volubly express gratitude for the chairman's injection of £1.2 million into the club coffers during the period of his involvement.

When, shortly afterwards, Watford were in a position to repay the interest-free loan after the sale of star players, Elton declined the offer on the grounds that the club's need was greater than his own.

'I loaned the money in the first place to give the club a good base and help them become not only a first division team but a club with a first division stadium. We have become a first division team but the rest is still to be completed.'

Earlier in the promotion campaign, Elton had also recalled with amusement how financial advisers had urged him to put his money into property.

His rationale was: 'What possible pleasure can you get from looking at a block of flats or a row of houses? I'm getting all the pleasure in the world from watching what has been constructed here.'

Doubtless, that pleasure was enhanced by the gratitude Elton felt towards Graham Taylor for the healthy influence the down to earth manager had exerted on his life.

'I was going through a stage about two years ago when I was drinking quite heavily and letting myself go physically. Graham took one look at me and said: "Come round to my house tomorrow morning." I did, and he immediately took out a bottle of brandy and put it on the table in front of me. He said "Go on, open it, that's what you really want, isn't it?" In that second, I saw what I was doing to myself and pulled myself together.'

The involvement with the football club had, in Britain, altered his status. Elton noted without irony that whereas in bygone years he was thought of by the general public as the superstar who owned a football club, the current perception was of the Watford chairman who had just brought out a record.

Though not quite in tandem with the accomplishments of his football team, *Jump Up* predicated a musical revival, for which no small credit was attributable to producer, Chris Thomas, on his first LP in sole command.

Keeping the producer very much in the family (Steve Brown, Gus Dudgeon, Clive Franks), had tended to make continuity a virtue at the expense of progression. The hits' collections aside, no album had satisfied any exacting criteria since *Goodbye Yellow Brick Road* in 1973.

That considered, there was scant element of risk in the introduction of Thomas – fresh from the contrasting milieu of incisive new wavers, the Pretenders. Anyway, he had already served an apprenticeship within the organization on *The Fox*.

In essence, the status quo was maintained, *Jump Up* containing the standard amalgam of ballads and the non-threateningly boisterous.

Yet the album not only exuded a sense of urgency lacking in its immediate predecessors – in 'Blue Eyes', it afforded Elton's best single in aeons.

With the now standard misreading of public taste, Elton could not be persuaded of the potential in the track, to the point of questioning its inclusion on the album. Yet the insistence of Chris Thomas – especially concerning the manner of the song's recording – reaped due reward.

Another from the stable of Gary Osborne's lightweight lyrics, 'Blue Eyes' was resuscitated by consummate melody and vocals bordering on the deadpan. A top ten record in Britain, a close call in America.

Further advances were in the pipeline as Elton worked on the follow-up album, *Too Low For Zero*. But the recording schedule was subject to interruption as Watford astounded the pundits by leading the first division. The band was kept waiting on the Caribbean island of Montserrat as Elton cancelled his plane ticket to enable him to sit nervously through fixtures against Swansea and West Bromwich.

Whatever his recording future held in store, the malaise at Rocket Records had reached crisis point. If Kiki Dee had felt the label insufficiently 'hungry' when departing in the late 1970s, it was now in the throes of terminal starvation.

The announcement considered inevitable in the industry came in the autumn. With the exception of Elton, all remaining Rocket artists would be dropped from the roster. In consequence, there would also be a pruning of staff.

With Elton again *in absentia* at a crisis stage, it was left to Rocket's managing director, John Hall, to deal with the press, relaying the star's sadness at the situation, particularly the redundancies of those who had long served the operation conscientiously.

In nine years, the label had not been starved of success – Kiki, Judie Tzuke, Blue and Neil Sedaka had charted on one or both sides of the Atlantic. Colin Blunstone and Randy Edelman were among others involved along the way.

Yet, as the cynics had envisaged, the label's resources largely depended on the vicissitudes of Elton's recording life.

Only the 1976 duet with Kiki had emulated the sales garnered during his peak period of 1973–75, when he was still contracted to DJM.

Elton could maintain his own career while simultaneously fulfilling an active role at Watford. But running a record company at the same time was really asking too much.

At the year's inception, John McEnroe was being talked about as a potential Rocket signing. If that was a foretaste of the future, the sensible option had been pursued.

Close on the heels of the enforcedly slimline Rocket came a pronouncement which shocked the family of the man he had once described as being like a father – 'a straight, right down the middle publisher' he would choose to have on his side in preference to anyone else . . . Dick James.

A statement from the singer confirmed that a writ had been issued against the Dick James business empire, seeking the return of copyrights to John–Taupin songs and a sum of damages in regard to earnings during the DJM era. The statement was the precursor to a lengthy legal battle which brought minuscule pleasure to any of the combatants.

Notwithstanding the strained atmosphere when Elton neared completion of his DJM contract, he had kept friendly, if irregular, contact with Dick and Stephen James over the intervening years.

The James family found it difficult to conceive that John Reid was not the prime mover behind the writ. And whatever the explanations offered by the plaintiffs for a seven year hiatus before bringing the action, it was impossible to ignore its institution just months after the conclusion of a comparable case.

Gilbert O'Sullivan – whose chart breakthrough in Britain had preceded Elton's by a matter of weeks – won a major High Court victory in May 1982 against former manager, Gordon Mills, and his company, Management Agency and Music Limited (MAM).

After hearing that O'Sullivan had received only about £500,000 of an estimated £14.5 million grossed by his records, Mr Justice Mars-Jones set aside agreements between the singer, Mills and MAM on the criterion of 'unreasonable restraint of trade'. The judge also ordered an inquiry into the profits made from the various agreements to ascertain the level of recompense to the singer.

O'Sullivan was awarded copyright of his songs, the master tapes of his records and costs estimated at £100,000.

The precedent having been established, the industry nervously awaited the next luminary to seek legal redress against a former company. Three months had elapsed since the judgement when Elton's statement provided the answer.

The pronouncement of future unpleasantries out of the way, a more positive focus was promised by Elton's return to the British stage, a major tour in November and December culminating in a staggering fourteen nights at the Hammersmith Odeon.

Sartorially, the advance word was to expect a grandiose general-issimo's outfit redolent of those worn by banana republic dignitaries in Marx Brothers movies.

The work of Californian designer, Bob Mackie, Elton described it as 'my Lord Choc-Ice outfit (after a favourite pseudonym), because it's so silly'. His alternative wardrobe for the forty-two concerts was equally heavy on the eyes.

North London constumier to the celebrities, John Kaye, contributed this little conservative number: a copacabana ensemble comprising a tutti-frutti coloured shirt and trousers, topped with headgear awash with fake fruit. A more traditional combination offered a huntsman's outfit with illuminating foxes on the shoulders.

Resplendent though he may have looked on stage in the run-up to the protracted Hammersmith finale, the suspicion was of yet another instance of Elton taking too much upon himself. Nevertheless, Hammersmith held happy memories for the performer.

At the peak of his popularity, two successive festive seasons at the venue ranked among his finest concert hours. An added virtue was the intimacy it afforded between artist and audience – 'it's not like Wembley, which is so vast that it is difficult to get a good atmosphere.'

It was precisely that close proximity which put Elton back in a negative spotlight.

The end of the tour was in sight when exhaustion and frustration heralded an explosive re-emergence of superstar pique.

Back to the basic band composition, Elton made no attempt to conceal his displeasure at the absence of Nigel Olsson behind the drum-kit at one Hammersmith concert through what was sub-sequently disclosed as a bout of gastric flu.

Audience members maintained that a sour demeanour permeated his remarks between numbers. But the real trouble was sparked off by the ritual throwing of the piano stool during 'Bennie And The Jets'.

The expected practice was for Elton to wield the seat in the direction of the back of the stage. On this night, however, he hurled the stool in a forward motion. It bounced off the orchestra pit and hit a girl seated in the front row of the stalls.

Elton was heard to exclaim to the injured party: 'If you're so hurt, why don't you get an RSPCA man,' before regaining his composure and summoning assistance for the girl. He then exited for a considerable time before returning to complete the performance.

Although the girl was more shocked than hurt, the incident negated much of the goodwill built up during the tour. Elton did make amends through an apology to the victim and an invite for her to attend the end of tour party at the Xenon nightclub.

By all accounts, she was one of the few to be granted an audience with the surly star, who closeted himself away from a celebrity cast list before departing in high dudgeon.

Completing a year of extremes, a song titled 'Princess' singularly failed to capture the imagination of the public, despite its Royal connotations. Gary Osborne said that Elton had written the melody with Princess Di in mind. In turn, his lyrics could be interpreted either as a guy serenading his girl or with specific application to the Prince of Wales, although first names were not mentioned.

Not that Elton could long eschew regal involvement. Pictured back in America in the company of actress, Samantha Eggar, he was a guest at the showbiz gala at Twentieth Century Fox attended by the Queen.

In the summer of 1983, Elton exultantly told the world of 'the most enjoyable trip I've been on for a long time'. The itinerary was free of concert and recording dates and the options for an opulent lifestyle were limited. It was just Elton, the Watford squad and innumerable quizzical onlookers on a prestigious footballing tour of China.

As in Russia four years previously, the star exhibited a genuine interest in the country and its culture. For him, it was a welcome novelty to be able to visit a famous landmark – the Great Wall – as an unabashed tourist without fear of being mobbed.

Further evidence of Elton's refined taste in *objets d'art* was shown in his £50,000 worth of purchases from an export warehouse near Peking. An escorted shopping expedition was arranged by his hosts after he had made known his interest in antiques.

With Watford winning their fixtures against the Chinese national team, the star even felt moved to give an impromptu concert at the hotel near Peking where the party was staying.

Elsewhere, he was back in the news for his music. Montserrat had proved the studio change most conducive to Elton's writing since the Chateau D'Herouville over a decade previously.

Removed from the attentions of both press and the showbiz set, Elton had come up with *Too Low For Zero* – his most convincing album since the mid 1970s. Nor did it pass without comment that this was the first true John–Taupin LP since *Blue Moves* in 1976 and that it was recorded with the original line-up of Dee, Nigel and Davey.

With Chris Thomas continuing as producer, the songs stood any comparative test with the output of the new generation of pretty pretty pop stars. Worldwide, the singles emanating from the LP won him a new generation of fans – and deservedly so.

The track with the strongest commercial impact was 'I Guess That's Why They Call It The Blues'. Reputedly laid down in a solitary take, it was the consummate slow burner.

'I'm Still Standing' was a wry statement of record, the lyrics depicting a true survivor who is an adolescent at heart. 'Kiss The Bride', the most cogent rocker, was to assume greater relevance in view of a surprise forthcoming event. The cause of the unexpected happening, Renate Blauel, had worked on the album, being credited among the list of 'special thanks'.

With the addition of 'Cold As Christmas (In The Middle Of The Year)', Elton enjoyed four domestic hits during 1983, a feat he last accomplished nine years previously.

In the resultant glow of acclaim, the star even presaged the resuscitation of projects deemed long moribund – for example, the 'Road' genre movie with Rod Stewart.

The friendship of Elton and Rod bore all the hallmarks of a turbulent marriage. At present everything was rosy, the duo taking exceptional pleasure in framing schoolboy poses for the tabloid photographers at a party for Liza Minnelli during her Victoria Palace season. Why, there might even be a place for little Liza in the movie. First, however, there was the small matter of a joint worldwide concert tour, commencing in Sydney next year.

'It's something we've been working on for a long time,' Elton explained. 'I want to do a two hour show with Rod which will feature both our bands.'

All too soon, though, the tour was off. Ditto for the movie and, in the short-term, the friendship amid bitter recrimination through the same popular media. Stage managed or otherwise, it was all immensely childish.

Two films Elton did shoot during this period of resurgence were courtesy of Russell Mulcahy, the video guru to the stars.

A decade too late for 'Crocodile Rock' and other likely candidates, the promotional film was an expensive new fact of music industry life, encouraged by the global proliferation of cable networks with time on their hands and insufficient programming to remove it.

Whereas in Britain, the outlets for the televising of pop videos were few and far between, the establishment of the American 24–hour music cable channel. MTV, had opened up a significant avenue of exposure.

For new British acts, it afforded a chance to crack the world's most lucrative market without recourse to arduous touring. For the well-known, it offered a gilt-edged opportunity. With the resources to fund the most exotic films, they were virtually guaranteed extensive showings, irrespective of the merits of the music.

With hindsight, it was hardly coincidental that new heart was breathed into the careers of listing rock 'n' roll dinosaurs as the fledgling cable channel changed the listening and viewing habits of millions of young middle-class Americans.

The Mulcahy video for 'I'm Still Standing' was prime-time cable fodder, not to mention an unsurpassable advertising campaign for the Cannes tourist authorities.

Dance movie clichés are effectively employed as an exuberant Elton is shown on the beach in some exceedingly fit company. Blink and a viewer miss the transient glimpse of a clapperboard bearing the slogan that said it all – 'Choc Ice lives'.

Divergently, the video for 'I Guess That's Why They Call It The Blues', also filmed in the South of France, finds Elton in a performance mode against the backdrop of a vignette owing a debt of inspiration to both *That'll Be The Day* and *An Officer And A Gentleman*. From Elton's standpoint, the highlight must have been the excuse to don a Jerry Lee Lewis outfit, hairpiece and all.

Lord Choc Ice lives indeed.

'Marriage is out for me and so are children. But I
can't predict anything. In ten years time I could
be married to Shirley Maclaine and we could
have six dwarfs' (*Elton John*, 1978).

The bridal couple met in a recording studio. The bride was a shy
German-born recording engineer. The groom was a flamboyant rock star who'd once said he wanted to marry — but
would not mind whether it was to a girl or boy.

Renate Blauel turned down a first proposal, made on the Caribbean
island of Montserrat, where they were working on Elton's *Breaking
Hearts* album. Three weeks later, the question was popped once more
over dinner at the Sebel Town House Hotel in Sydney.

In the description of personal assistant, and bridesmaid, Patti
Mostyn: 'It was just after midnight. Elton was having a lingering dinner
alone with her and I was sitting in the lounge with John Reid and a
couple of members of his band. They came in hand-in-hand and
announced the news. Elton looked over the moon.'

Two of the first recipients of the wedding plans were Watford's
manager, Graham Taylor, and record producer, Clive Franks, who
remembered being woken up by a long distance telephone call from
the groom to be. 'He rang me to say, "I'm getting married to Renate." I
was half-asleep and said, "You're kidding." It was such a shock.'

Kiki Dee was similarly surprised. 'The press somehow got hold of my
number and rang to ask if it was true. It was a complete shock.
Everyone was taken aback.

'His friends knew Renate in a professional capacity. She had worked
with Elton and, in fact, engineered a track of mine, "The Loser Gets To
Win". But marriage?'

Only Bernie Taupin publicly failed to share in the atmosphere of amazement – although it was a month after the happy event.

'We all expected his marriage,' the lyricist proclaimed. 'You know he's not really any different. He's just just an ordinary guy with a football team and a pint in his hand.'

Back at the Sebel Town House, it was a case of 'don't call us, we'll call you'. Elton was incommunicado to the world's press at his luxury base which, four days later, was to host the wedding reception.

Naturally, there was the obligatory last-minute hitch. Prospective marrieds in New South Wales had to wait thirty days for a licence, unless there were extenuating circumstances.

Predictably, New South Wales Attorney-General, Paul Landa, was not a man to bar the path to true love – or a massive publicity boost for his State.

A professed Elton fan, he gave the union his secular blessing as the media circus rolled into town, explaining that the prohibitive statute only existed to protect couples from the possible consequences of youthful impetuosity.

So 14 February it was. Every aspect of the event was a gift to catchline writers the world over. A St Valentine's Day ceremony; a church in the suburb of Darling Point and a groom fresh from the charts with a hit single titled 'Kiss The Bride'. The *Daily Mirror* perhaps offered the most exotic summary, describing the future Elton and Renate John as 'Megastar and his Prussian possum'.

The day went off well. Both the bride and groom were dressed in white for the ceremony in the tiny St Mark's Church. A crowd of 2,000 cheered as Renate was escorted up the steps in her traditional wedding gown and long veil. Exercising the bride's prerogative, Renate was three minutes late for her marriage. Elton was seventeen minutes early.

Emerging arm-in-arm after the service, the newlyweds proceeded to the £50,000 reception attended by 100 guests, for which Elton changed into a blue suit.

Michael and Mary Parkinson, Janet Street Porter, Barry Humphries and Olivia Newton-John were among those who enjoyed a wedding feast of prawns, smoked salmon, oysters, scallops, lamb, beef, stuffed quail, trout, turkey and chicken, accompanied by fine wines and the finest champagne.

The most original alleged telegram was said to be courtesy of Michael Jackson: 'I had to burn my hair to get on the front page–you got married.'

Close friend, Billy Gaff, dispensed with the niceties, his congratulatory message reading: 'You may still be standing but the rest of us are on the floor!'

Most notable among the absent friends was Elton's mother and stepfather, Fred, who watched the wedding at their West Sussex home through a TV link-up.

Sheila was delighted at the marriage and the talk was of a 'second wedding' in London in the spring. Although she had not met Renate, she felt that Elton had made a prudent choice.

'She's thirty and not some slip of a girl of seventeen, which is what I first feared. She seems that sort of girl who will keep Elton in his place.'

As for the type of domestic living Renate could anticipate, Sheila Farebrother was explicit. 'Elton is sensible and likes home life. Most of all he loves children, and I don't think he'll waste any time making sure he gets some.'

Her son confirmed these sentiments a few days after the wedding. Asked to predict Watford's chances in a crucial fixture, he responded that he never forecasted football results. 'But I can predict that we are going to start a family.'

The union had got off to a blessed start with Watford continuing their cup progress, the groom deserting the marital bed in New Zealand (where the newlyweds were now encamped) to phone England for news in the wee small hours.

When they arrived back from the antipodes in early April, the couple's monogrammed luggage spoke more eloquently than a torrent of press quotes. Some thirty pieces stood together. Half bore the initials 'EHJ', the others 'RB'.

But on reflection, Elton did have this to say for the benefit of the media hounds: 'I never really had any thought of getting married, but suddenly, "bang!" After thirty-seven years I found someone I wanted to marry.'

And as to the prospective lifestyle of Mr and Mrs Elton Hercules John: 'We are not going to be a couple who go out to discos – I'm tired of them anyway – and dinner parties. We just want to spend some time together. We want to have a home life.'

In direct contradiction, Elton launched himself into one of those hectic spells, which in less contented circumstances, might have been viewed as inadvisable.

Complementing his personal and football fortunes, his records were again on a high. Sung by Elton, 'recorded by Renate', with Chris

Thomas remaining at the production helm, *Breaking Hearts* provided commercial evidence that *Too Low For Zero* was more than an isolated pocket of resistance.

The album spawned three major hits in America, two in Britain.

Montserrat was the perfect recording environment for 'Passengers', a jaunty calypso number. The formulaic poignant ballad – and not a million miles in structure from 'Bennie And The Jets' – 'Sad Songs (Say So Much)' encouraged *déjà vu* in another sense. With the exception of *Victim Of Love*, it could have been accommodated quite cogently on every studio album since 1973.

Amidst the more familiar haunts of Sweden, Germany and Holland, his post-nuptial tour broke new geographical ground. Five years after Russia, Elton returned to the Eastern bloc with a commensurately newsworthy slant.

Concerts in Poland were of trivial import to Western media correspondents when weighed against Elton's informal meeting with the country's most recognizable global personality.

A passion for soccer was a common denominator between the extrovert rock star and the charismatic Solidarity figurehead, Lech Walesa. A one-hour-get-together in Gdansk also embraced discussion of politics and computers, as well as the exchange of autographs and gifts. Further illustration of Elton's standing as a rock 'n' roll diplomat was his tennis match with the American ambassador in Czechoslovakia.

Politics of another description were rumoured to be the motivation behind Elton's conspicuous absence from the Montreux Pop Festival the following month. Although the official word was that a missed air connection had precluded his appearance, the backstage gossip was that he had withdrawn because of a dispute over billing. Perhaps the truth of the matter was that his mind was focussed on events nearer home...

Elton's first competitive appearance at Wembley Stadium in 1975 had resulted in an away defeat. Topping a bill sprinkled liberally with musical luminaries, it was his misfortune to follow on stage a near perfect greatest hits rendition from the Beach Boys – and a miscalculation to preview the *Captain Fantastic* LP in its entirety.

With Watford a fourth division outfit at the time, a triumphant footballing return within a decade seemed unthinkable.

Yet in 1984, with press attention centred on Elton's surprise marriage, Watford stealthily progressed towards football's showpiece occasion. A side shrewdly assembled by Graham Taylor despatched local rivals, Luton, before dispensing with Charlton, Brighton, Birmingham and Plymouth.

With Wembley beckoning – and the illustrious Everton to conquer – frantic arrangements were made to ensure Elton's arrival, which involved interrupting a German tour. After playing in Essen on the preceding night, he was whisked back to England in the early hours, well in time for the kick-off.

The event was the culmination of a dream for this unlikeliest of football club chairmen. In a fraternity rivalling the theatre for its superstitious ephemera, great store was laid by Elton's touring absence for the rounds leading to the final. Jinx or no jinx, he sat with Renate in the Royal Box and made an emotional spurt on to the pitch at the end of the game. It seemed almost immaterial that Watford had lost 2 – 0, the crucial counter being allowed by the referee despite what neutral observers felt to be a foul on goalkeeper, Steve Sherwood, by the scorer, Andy Gray.

Elton later described his pitch invasion as 'an emotional once-in-a-lifetime experience. I have played in front of 450,000 people in New York's Central Park and had other crowds of 200,000. But this was something else.'

He added: 'Though disappointed with the result, I thoroughly enjoyed myself. Both sets of fans were fantastic.'

It did not escape the lenses of the accredited photographers that Renate looked suspiciously happy when Everton scored. His wife had a lot to learn about the game, Elton explained. Nor did it go unnoticed that the Wembley electronic scoreboard carried an apposite advertisement for 'Sad Songs (Say So Much)'. Ostentation is business.

The scoreline in no way affected plans for a lavish post–match party at the home of John Reid.

With a disco in one elegant marquee and a full orchestra in another, 260 guests, the Watford players among them, danced the night away. Elton's now standard finale saw him joined by Kiki Dee for 'Don't Go Breaking My Heart' – a distressing selection for any party-goer still capable of remembering the events at Wembley. 'I would have sung it whether we had won or lost,' Elton admitted. Anyway, having presided over Watford's rise from the Football League basement to first division runners-up and cup finalists in successive years, he could at least celebrate the confirmation of the club's place in the top strata.

Kiki's own recollection was that while initially disheartened, Elton rapidly reverted to a sense of pride in Watford's achievement. 'It was at times like this that you could see that the club was the stabilizing influence he needed. It was very down to earth, no bullshit. It was like being a million miles away from the music business.'

The party over, it was back to business. Attending his team's ceremonial parade through Watford, he barely had time for a farewell drink at the town hall reception before being spirited away for a flight to Germany to resume his concert schedule in Hamburg.

But he left determined to do all in his powers to ensure that the glory days would continue at Vicarage Road. 'Things can really take off from now,' he declared. 'We have a young team and the future looks good. My function is to get the stadium in order, because we have got a fourth division ground. But we can't have a white elephant. It's no use having a super stadium if the team is poor – and that won't be allowed to happen.'

Within three years, the club had reached another FA Cup semi-final, was comfortably ensconced in the upper echelons of the first division, had successfully pioneered family enclosures – and opened a £2.2 million stand.

It was the sort of entreprenurial accomplishment which echoed the credo of the British Prime Minister – who would have been further impressed has she been briefed on Elton's school election campaign.

Although the star's irregular political quotes hardly suggested an affinity with the Conservative Party, one doesn't turn down an invitation to lunch at Chequers with Margaret Thatcher.

Between two diners of implacable resolve, polite discussion might conceivably have encompassed how Elton finally won at Wembley.

After the consecutive losses to the Beach Boys and Everton, Elton had returned to the famous stadium six weeks after the cup final to headline a concert co-sponsored by Radio One.

Following the eclectic talents of Nik Kershaw, Big Country and Kool And The Gang, he gave a masterful show, topped by an elongated version of 'Bennie And The Jets'.

Offstage, the star was attempting a period of transition. Mindful of the responsibilities of the newly married, Elton was espied less frequently at parties during the summer. Instead, he escorted Renate to West End theatre – musicals, naturally.

First nighters for 42nd Street at the Theatre Royal Drury Lane, they also made it to *Little Shop Of Horrors*, the cult American hit about a plant with an appetite both unusual and unhealthy.

A romantic sojourn saw the couple cruising the Mediterranean in Elton's yacht. Back on shore, the honeymoon was over. America awaited, with the usual inexpedient touring schedule.

E lton's entrance to the 1985 Montreux Rock Festival was short but sweet. He stayed just long enough in the picturesque venue to perform for a BBC Rock Special his first duet since Kiki Dee and France Gall.

'Act Of War' was a song written by him and Bernie with Tina Turner in mind. Her career in renaissance, Tina could afford to be gracious in rejection.

Undaunted, the writers learnt that the raunchy Millie Jackson was coming to Britain for concerts and decided to try and interest her in the song. Not one to let the grass grow under his feet, Elton arranged for a tape to be presented to 'the female Richard Pryor' when she arrived at Heathrow Airport.

Though hardly the ideal repository for much of Elton's material, Millie liked 'Act Of War' and agreed to recording sessions being woven around her live commitments.

Two extravagant stage performers could hardly fail to come up with an appealing promotional film – and they did.

The White House hoves into view. A State Department official is on the hotline, fingers itching to depress the red button at his side: 'Oh, hello Mr President . . . What's that? . . . Elton John with Millie Jackson . . . You want to get him in sixty?'

Evocative stuff. And the visuals continue to excite as Elton and Millie's war game culminates amid the debris. They go out in full voice.

Alas, it was one of those instances of 'nice video, shame about the song'. There was more than a grain of truth in Elton's jest that by comparison, Millie made him 'sound like Andy Pandy'.

'Act Of War' was quickly forgotten. What grew from Bob Geldof's reaction to a horrific TV news report about famine in Africa would long be remembered.

Elton met Geldof at the Ivor Novello awards, where he was collecting an honour for Band Aid's 'Do They Know It's Christmas' single.

While attracting some of the superstar cast for the historic Live Aid was the stuff that ulcers are made of, the Irishman required none of his well documented abrasive charisma to obtain Elton's services. Apprised of the project, he immediately agreed to participate.

To his manager's credit, John Reid was quickly on the phone to Geldof to inquire whether there was any way his office could assist in the organization of the event. He was told that his most telling contribution would be to inform other managers of Elton's ready acceptance.

A date for the annals of rock 'n' roll history is 13 July 1985.

On both sides of the Atlantic, Live Aid brought together the rock hierarchy – Bowie, Collins, Jagger, McCartney, Dylan – with a plethora of young pretenders. One of the latter was George Michael, who had outgrown the youthful Wham image and was moving inexorably towards a solo career.

Elton's slot was scheduled at the climax of a magical day of entertainment at Wembley Stadium that will remain in the memory of those fortunate enough to have obtained tickets and the countless millions worldwide who watched on television.

Introduced by Billy Connolly as 'a friend of mine from planet Windsor,' Elton made his customary bedazzling entrance in a shimmering red and striped ensemble, topped off with an example of the Cossack headgear he had favoured of late.

For those enamoured of keeping abreast with the alterations in his band, there was much to assimilate. Davey and Ray represented the stalwarts, there being no sign of Dee and Nigel.

David Paton, once of teeny-orientated hit-makers, Pilot, had taken over the bassist's duties. Fred Mandel was on keyboards, Charlie Morgan on drums. The line-up was further augmented by a heavy-weight brass section and a backing quartet including Kiki Dee. Now that is what is known as a real rock 'n' roll band.

What followed should have put an end to all argument over what sort of accompaniment (if any), Elton should utilize for live engagements. From the instantly recognizable opening bars of 'I'm Still Standing', the global audience witnessed a truncated stage show as good in its way as the earlier concert encapsulations of Queen and U2, which were jointly acknowledged as the apogee of the British segment.

'Bennie And The Jets' sounded as vibrant as ever; 'Rocket Man' was the cue for a mass arm swaying by those watching from the vantage point of the stadium pitch.

Then came the Elton announcement generating the greatest response since he welcomed John Lennon on stage at Madison Square Garden.

'I am gonna introduce a friend of mine . . . He's going to sing one of my songs . . . This guy I admire very much for his musical talent. . .'

Come in George Michael, a vision in black.

Wham comrade, Andrew Ridgeley, was consigned to the chorus line as George too addressed the masses.

He got as far as: 'This is one of my favourite tracks of Elton's. . .' before the glittering one led his band into 'Don't Let The Sun Go Down On Me'.

With inclement sense of occasion, the heavens defied the message of the song by opening for the first time during the day. The shower soon subsided but its effect on the intricate electrical equipment was said to have been a factor in Paul McCartney's subsequent silent start to 'Let It Be'.

Both George and Elton having publicly expressed admiration for the other's accomplishments, their Wembley partnership was more than the result of felicitous programming.

According to Kiki Dee, George Michael additionally made a telling off-stage contribution.

'When Elton rang me excitedly to say that he had been allotted thirty minutes at Live Aid, he said he had already asked George to do a song with him.

'For our own part, Elton and I had planned to duet on 'Dancing In The Street' before discovering that Bowie and Jagger had beaten us to it.

'So there we were, trying desperately to think of something new and different, while George insisted: "Do something the public wants to hear." In the end, he persuaded us to stick with "Don't Go Breaking My Heart".'

He was a good judge of audience character. The song went down a storm.

Having enhanced his reputation with another generation of pop fans, Elton was shortly back on a now intensively populated stage for the grand finale of 'Do They Know It's Christmas'. When last espied, he was straining to get at the microphone guarded by Adam Ant, Big Country and Roger Daltrey.

George Michael was one of many in the vanguard of the new order of pop to pay tribute to Elton's work. For them, unlike their punk predecessors, there was no embarrassment in the admission.

Musically, there was much common ground between Elton and artists like Michael and Boy George. Furthermore, many of their teenage followers were also Elton fans, having first been exposed to his music through the *Too Low For Zero* album.

In the manner that Elton was in awe of John Lennon, having grown up through the Beatles' era, the chart class of 1985 held Elton in reverential regard, associating him with the music of their own adolescence.

George Michael and Elton again teamed up during the year on an original hit – 'Wrap Her Up' (from Elton's new album, *Ice On Fire*) as well as for a video and further concert appearances.

Also featured on the LP was another emergent talent thought highly of by the old stager – Nik Kershaw, who had been on the same Wembley Stadium bill for the 1984 Radio One concert.

In common with many of the Live Aid stars, Elton latterly found fresh attention focussed upon his music. Considering his innumerable charitable gestures over the years, he was a deserving benefactor.

With the stadium extravaganza behind him, Elton offered his services to a less publicized charity bash. Along with Pete Townshend and Imagination, he gave a concert in St James's Park in aid of handicapped children and drug addicts. Roger Moore and Anthony Andrews were among a select audience for the concert and an accompanying auction.

But at the end of the year, charity reverted to his loyal fans as Elton returned to his old stamping ground of Wembley Arena for a series of pre-Christmas shows.

Lest anyone have forgotten the impending festivities, Elton supplied a characteristically subtle hint by taking the stage in a two-foot high bouffant wig flashing the greeting, 'Merry Xmas'.

Yet by past standards, the remainder of the proceedings might genuinely be described as decorous.

Planted behind an enormous white piano, Elton led the thirteen-piece band nurtured since Live Aid through what *The Times* reviewer saw as 'a near faultless rendering of a tiny proportion of his vast repertoire, complemented by vibrant synchronized lighting changes and a clear, precise PA sound.'

Maintaining the star's Royal connections, Princess Diana and Prince Andrew not only attended one of the Wembley shows but graced a post-concert backstage party.

Ice On Fire had added two new options to Elton's concert hit parade.

'Nikita' – featuring George Michael on backing vocals and Nik Kershaw on guitar – undoubtedly satisfied the section of his following who, as told to talk show hosts, would implore the singer: 'Why don't you make another proper record like "Daniel"?'

A song for Russia, Ken Russell's surprisingly restrained video depicts 'Nikita' as a lustrous blonde border guard with whom Elton becomes infatuated when driving his Rolls-Royce through a Soviet border control.

In a subsequent dream sequence, both director and artist get to reminisce about *Tommy* as Elton takes 'Nikita' to a Watford game wearing the gargantuan boots he sported so manfully as the Pinball Wizard.

'Nikita' was Elton's biggest domestic solo hit for thirteen years, getting to number three in the BBC charts. A major factor in its failure to reach the pinnacle was the year's top seller, 'The Power Of Love', recorded by 'that silly girl, Jennifer Rush', an imminent singing partner.

'Wrap Her Up' – the second hit from the LP – was little more than a slimline 'Bite Your Lip', flavoured with a video showing both George Michael's flair for the medium and an exotic montage of leading ladies, among them Marilyn Monroe and Joan Collins.

The closing segment invokes the names of leading ladies as incongruous as Samantha Fox. Kiki Dee materializes in person at the mention of her name, only to be rewarded with a custard pie from point blank range.

With George Michael a hot ticket Stateside, Geffen chose to release 'Wrap Her Up' in advance of 'Nikita' for the US market. Taste prevailed as 'Nikita' attained the higher chart placing.

In February of 1986, taste was a commodity in short supply when the annual British Phonographic Industry awards designated a special accolade to Elton, ostensibly for having gone to Russia seven years previously.

Norman Tebbit made a frightening fist of his unaccustomed role as avuncular presenter. The acceptance speech, evoking thinly concealed distaste, completed a compelling cameo for the large television audience.

Livid at being used for what he considered a superficial purpose, Elton's temper quickly reached boiling point once he was off camera. Back in the privacy of his suite, he put his award through some strenuous target practice. The fragments did not accompany him to Windsor.

His anger at the farcical BPI honour had abated by April when he was the proud recipient of two awards at another central London ceremony. At the Ivor Novello presentations he was summoned to the dais to collect awards for outstanding service to British music and for the year's best song ('Nikita').

While assuaging the assembled luminaries by declaring that the Ivor Novello awards were those that meant the most, Elton did retain a pointed footnote for the waiting media: 'The only award worth having is a gold disc – that means people have bought your record.'

In America, the public had unreservedly been purchasing a new Elton hit, with one crucial difference. In this instance Elton was not the star of the piece, but one of three legendary 'Friends' of Dionne Warwick, supporting the songstress on 'That's What Friends Are For' – a record whose proceeds benefited research into Aids. Elton's first anonymous number one, his friends in the chorus were Gladys Knight and Stevie Wonder.

Altruism is a quality rarely associated with the music industry, many of those generating profits into multiple figures being curmudgeonly by-words.

How fierce, one speculates, would the stampede for Live Aid participation have been without an assured global television audience of millions of potential record buyers?

Yet Elton transcends all this. From the earliest days, he has made generous provision to preferred charities, while directing concert proceeds towards predestined beneficiaries.

Outsiders might contend that Elton can well afford to be munificent. The truth is, of course, that he does not have to be.

So when he periodically displays the questionable McEnroe-type temperament of a music brat, it is as well to weigh the negative impression against the manifold examples of the obverse side of his character.

Charity is not merely about writing out a cheque. It is the expression of a genuinely caring attitude about others.

Down the years, loyal Watford footballers have swelled their testimonial earnings through a specially arranged concert by Elton. Yet Keith Mercer had left the club five years before injury terminated his career when at Blackpool.

He knew that Elton had kept abreast of his achievements: 'I met him annually at the Player of the Year dinner, to which I was always invited as a past winner. He is the sort of chairman who keeps an eye out for players who have contributed to Watford's success when they move on to other clubs.'

More unexpected was how the star wholeheartedly supported his testimonial game at Blackpool. 'Not only did Watford provide the opposition. To make the match, Elton had to fly in by private plane to the local airport. It had to be kept open for him.

'Four thousand people attended that game and Elton patiently signed every autograph requested. His involvement made the night. It was a wonderful gesture and typical of the man. I haven't a bad word to say about him.'

If Elton essayed a parternalistic trait towards footballers bereft of fortune, close friends were touched more by simple gestures than obscenely generous tokens.

Kiki Dee – now navigating a new professional course as an actress – was appearing in the Western influenced West End musical, *Pump Boys and Dinettes*, with other industry absconders, Paul Jones, Gary Holton and Carlene Carter.

Just as Elton had made a point of being present at Kiki's first night gigs, he had scheduled a free evening for her last performance in *Pump Boys* before a cast changeover. As is standard when Elton is among a concert audience, he did not remain in his seat for the duration.

A memorable cameo from the show is the moment when a seat number is called out from the stage. The occupant then has the dubious privilege of joining the cast to pick a prize for a spoof raffle victory.

With prodigious cast collusion, Elton was ordained the lucky winner and bounced up to claim his just deserts.

Said Kiki: 'The prize was a choice from three air fresheners – bikini, skunk and Christmas tree. Though I can't remember which one Elton chose, knowing him, it must have been bikini.'

As for material gifts, Kiki has been on the receiving end of dresses from Browns costing thousands of pounds, a diamond ring from Cartier as a birthday present and, recently, 'an amazing coat of ostrich feathers. He joked that the wife didn't like it!'

He has continued to lavish presents on John Reid, among them a £30,000 clock, a Graham Sutherland painting and a Lamborghini. Each Christmas those in his first category of acquaintances receive the most exotic hampers from the Fortnum and Mason stocks.

Elton is commensurately generous when shopping for himself. A

Cartier chandelier for positioning over a swimming pool set him back a cool £150,000. He has expensive taste in cars vintage and ultra-modern, his collection augmented by a 1928 Melbourne tram which cost more to ship than to purchase.

A past festive season gift to himself was a television and video unit with a five-foot square screen. And his Monopoly set cost more than the acquisition of the most exclusive properties on the board.

Contained in a rosewood box are playing pieces of gold and silver. The hotel tokens are nine-carat gold and the houses are silver, replicating Georgian town dwellings.

Other purchases bring to mind with clarity the schoolboy archivist fighting a rearguard action against a parental campaign to consign a mountainous collection of football and concert programmes to the garage and/or refuse.

In 1981, Elton took great delight, and conspicuous pride, in the purchase, at Christie's, of Spike Milligan's 232 Goon Show scripts for the programmes broadcast between May 1951 and January 1960. A snip at £14,000, plus a 10 per cent premium.

The cynics could cavil at Elton's assertion of being a lifelong fan, exclaiming that he was a mere thirteen when the last show was broadcast.

Elton's riposte – in a passable Bluebottle imitation – was: 'I have boughted dem because I love dem.'

20

'I've been very lucky with DJM. It's a small
company where you can go in and say what you
want. It's like a home and family' (*Elton John* 1972).

For fifty days, the High Court provided an unfamiliar stage as
Elton, with Bernie Taupin, brought a costly action against the
organization which had given them their decisive break in the
business.

The duo were seeking redress on two fronts. They sought the return
of the copyrights to 144 songs – among them 'Rocket Man', 'Crocodile
Rock', 'Daniel' and 'Goodbye Yellow Brick Road' – and a bigger share of
the £200 million their early success generated.

In evidence, Elton had said that he was twenty and Bernie seventeen
when they signed up. The £50 advanced and £25 combined weekly
salary (Elton got £15, Bernie £10) 'seemed very fair to us at the time'.
After the release of the *Elton John* album in 1970, a substantial increase
in recording royalties was negotiated.

Dick James claimed to have made only £1.5 million profit from the
vast sums earned by Elton during the prolific DJM period. During the
same timespan, the singer received £13.4 million from his recording
contract, supplemented by a further £1 million plus from his publishing agreements.

It was also pointed out that Dick James retained the rights to many
unreleased John–Taupin compositions, which could reasonably be
assumed to include hit material.

There were no real victors when Mr Justice Nicholls delivered a
four-and-a-half-hour judgement. He ruled that the songwriting
partnership had been deliberately underpaid while under contract to
Dick James Music, the pair having signed a publishing, recording and
management deal in 1967 when they were 'young and inexperienced'.

Moreover, the duo had been awestruck at dealing with one of the giants of the music publishing industry and were desperate to be signed up by him.

Innocents in the business, they had relied on Dick James to ensure that the contractual terms were fair and reasonable.

The publishing contract, with no provision for the rate of royalties to be increased, was an 'unreasonably hard bargain'.

Elton and Bernie were entitled to monies made by overseas sub-publishing companies set up by DJM on royalties and 'excessive' fees charged by the company for making, producing and distributing Elton John records. The amount would take into account interest calculated from 1967.

But the claim on copyrights had been left too late. Dick James had given them their start and the plaintiffs had gone on to career success beyond their wildest dreams.

The judge stressed that Dick James had not consciously sought to gain an unfair advantage.

As is customary after such legal battles, both parties expressed themselves pleased with the judgement, putting the best respective interpretation on its effect.

Bernie Taupin told reporters: 'I feel proud. Everything we went in to prove, we proved. It is a moral victory.'

Elton, on tour in Edinburgh, shared his partner's sentiments. 'It's a pity about the copyrights but I think the judge handled it very fairly.'

His advice to newcomers to the business was 'to get a really good lawyer'.

A 'relieved and exhausted' Dick James would have been liable for £30 million had the copyright claim been upheld. Lawyers acting for the publisher estimated that the cost of the judgement to their client was £500,000.

The songwriters' legal team forecast that the ruling was worth considerably more – possibly up to £5 million. But Elton's annual earnings comfortably surpassed that figure. With costs estimated at £1.5 million, he was left to reflect on whether it had all really been worthwhile. As events transpired, probably not.

Dick James died two months later at the age of sixty-five. The strain to which he was subjected by the mammoth court case was thought to have been a contributory factor.

Elton's reaction was to agree to meet the legal costs incurred by James during the High Court action, reiterating that all personal claims against the duo's former boss had been dismissed by the judge.

Thereafter, Elton ensured that proper tribute was paid if the early days were discussed during interviews.

'Dick James was tremendous to me,' he now acknowledges unreservedly.

21

> 'I go out there and get every person in the
> building quiet when I sing a slow song and get
> them shouting their heads off when I do a fast
> one. It's giving 100 per cent of yourself. Even if I
> had a broken leg, I'd hop around on it for two-
> and-a-half hours if I had to' (Elton John on the
> joys of performance, 1976).

If Elton's twentieth anniversary in the music business got away to a volatile start, the calm before the storm was a triumphant return to America in 1986, no more so than at New York's Madison Square Garden.

It seemed hard to credit that twelve years had elapsed since Lennon made his last stage exit in present company. Particularly as with a red mohawk head-dress competing for attention with a black and silver cape, Elton and his eleven-piece band dazzled fans old and new alike with a volley of blasts from the past.

There was no possible comment from the fashion writers. Speaking on tour about his latterday attitude to stage wear, Elton declared: 'I don't do it to be outrageous. I do it because I like it. One year I made the top ten best dressed men and the top ten worst dressed women.'

In conciliatory fashion, the music critics had more to opine. The same *New York Times* writer who, seven years previously, had suggested that the star should be launched into Las Vegas orbit complimented Elton on now performing more to please himself than the audience that purchased his singles: 'The irony of this is that he is pleasing himself by recasting the songs in the rocking rhythm and blues mode he favoured early in his career and this is making them more exciting than ever – and pleasing the audience more. The crowd at the Garden was almost delirious with enthusiasm and had every right to be.'

At this point, Elton could justifiably effervesce about the kindness of Americans – 'the most generous people in the world.'

Likewise, the star was an avowed supporter of Australia and its lifestyle. A favourite port of call – its summer coinciding with the English winter – a priceless amenity of his Sydney base was a panoramic view of the famous harbour.

Before his throat trouble silenced him, if not the press, Elton had exorcised a past ghost–the memory of the 1971 concert with orchestra at the Royal Festival Hall, for which he believed the hired classical hands did not perform to their full potential.

The Melbourne Symphony Orchestra exhibited no such cultural snobbery in performances which provided the perfect showcase for the songs from the period of Paul Buckmaster arrangements.

'The only thing that really kept me going with the voice was the thought that I'd got to go on with the orchestral set,' he later confessed. But only just.

One date in Perth was cancelled and towards the end of his twenty-seven appearances, he collapsed on stage in Sydney. None the less, most audiences were quickly disabused of the notion that they had paid to see an ailing performer.

The band was largely the Live Aid model, featuring Davey, Ray, David Paton, Charlie Morgan, Fred Mandel, the four man brass section, plus Jody Linscott on percussion.

Most had featured on the year's studio release, *Leather Jackets*, posing in suitably evocative attire for the album sleeve.

Recorded in Holland, *Leather Jackets* saw the return of some familiar names. After an unheralded comeback on *Ice On Fire* – his first Elton assignment since *Blue Moves* – Gus Dudgeon was retained. A name from even farther back, Steve Brown was credited as co-ordinator.

Other acknowledgements of note were Cliff Richard – for the duet 'Slow Rivers' – Queen's Roger Taylor and John Deacon as guest players and Cher and Lady Choc Ice (Renate) for writing 'Don't Trust That Woman'.

Gus Dudgeon accompanied the touring party in Australia on sound duty, as did another stalwart, Clive Franks.

Just like old times, and that tends to be the preference of the artist. Explained Kiki Dee: 'Obviously, in such a long time in the business, you are bound to go through personnel changes. Everyone was surprised when Gus was brought back, but that's Elton. He enjoys working with people he feels comfortable with.'

It was 14 December 1986 at the Sydney Entertainment Centre. In a fortnight the press vultures would hover ravenously over the bones of a purportedly skeletal performing future. Tonight was one for the fans.

Sporting wig and earrings that would not look incongruous on a 'Dynasty' set, the first half was hits and more hits, albeit with varied interpretation. 'Rocket Man' encompassed 'Hey Jude', 'Bennie And The Jets' allowed for a spot of virtuoso piano from the Glenn Miller song catalogue.

The orchestra segment revealed the pianist in a white suit with glittering trim and waistcoat. Hair-wise the soap opera candidate had given way to an exemplary pastiche of The Great Composer's wig, the effect enhanced by a designer dimple.

With the enthusiastic support of the Melbourne Symphony musicians, Elton breezed through another programme of standards, allowing himself a few less populist inclusions. Orchestra or no orchestra, he still finished with 'Saturday Night's Alright'.

Elton had committed himself to the Australian itinerary in full cognizance of the likely consequences to his vocal health.

The first inkling of the problem had come in America, where he had to cancel the first two shows. Elton listened to medical advice from a variety of sources, but his intention was always to fulfil the Australian dates, because of their orchestral component.

'I kept back from people how bad it was,' he admitted. 'In Australia, I saw a specialist who said: "You shouldn't really be singing, but if you want to do the tour, that's up to you. Afterwards, I'm going to have you in and do the operation."'

In the event, Elton's fears of a more serious ailment proved groundless. The operation to strengthen the vocal chords was a relatively minor one, surgery being completed in fifteen minutes. Annie Lennox and Paul Young are among a host of other stars to have resumed singing after similar treatment. The only real cure is a rest from vocal work, an almost unthinkable self-denial for Elton.

It was difficult enough for him to contain himself as an audience member, as Kiki Dee could confirm from personal experience.

'Elton could never go to a concert without wanting to get up on stage. He'd be sitting edgily in his seat, then suddenly would disappear backstage. The next thing you knew, he would be up front making a guest appearance. He really used to enjoy that.'

Three years of almost continuous work had taken their toll. Now Elton was forced to concede that a period of non-playing sporting activity would not go amiss.

The good thing about being an Englishman in Australia during the 1986–87 cricket season was the miraculous form displayed by the touring team. For the first time in recent memory, England's cricketers had strung together a run of victories. With more time than customary on his hands, Elton had been elevated to the status of number one supporter.

The Australian TV cameras suggested almost a machiavellian involvement by the singer in England's triumphant trail in the tests and limited overs fixtures. If a Pommie reached a hundred, no sooner would his bat be raised to the crowd than the cameras would switch their attention to the stands, and an applauding Elton John. If Australian wickets began to tumble, ditto.

Mirroring events at Watford, a bond of mutual admiration developed between Elton and the England players. He entered hospital for his operation clutching good luck tokens presented to him by the squad.

After surgery, Elton readily acknowledged that the cricketer most likely to place unnecessary strain on his vocal chords was the roistering Ian Botham, a larger than life friend to complement other headline grabbers, Rod Stewart and Billie Jean King.

Better than anyone, Botham could empathize with Elton over harassment by sections of the popular media. But the superficially surprising alliance between the two goes far deeper.

The week after Elton's 'One To One' interview with Michael Parkinson was broadcast, viewers saw Botham on the same programme crediting the singer as being a major career influence. Furthermore, Elton was praised for being a source of comfort to the Botham family in troubled times.

'Elton I regard as one of my closest friends and, above all else, one of the nicest people I have met in my life... A great guy, very generous.'

Before departing from his regular Los Angeles sojourn the following summer, Elton made a point of catching Botham in action for his new team, Worcestershire, in a County Championship fixture with Leicester.

Renate not renowned as a great sporting fan, Elton took along a few other mates for company – Eric Clapton and George Harrison.

With Botham consigned to the field for the majority of play, the superstars were hosted by another acquaintance from the England tour – Leicestershire's David Gower.

Any free time was exhausted meeting the copious demands of autograph hunters.

Elton's Watford cap was again brought into service for the cricketing awayday. It was still perched securely over the remains of transplant number umpteen when he was spotted in the Heathrow departure lounge a few weeks later awaiting his LA flight.

Had ill-health not intervened, the visit would have been classified as a working one. The original intention was for Elton to play thirty-two American engagements, doubtless to be followed by concerts elsewhere.

At forty, he still retained an unquenchable zest to play for his fans. Before finally submitting to doctors' advice, he had given 200 performances in a timespan of frightening brevity. At the multi-million dollar end of the profession, such torture is simply not countenanced.

Naturally, this itinerant lifestyle has not been conducive to a stable domestic existence, as evidenced by his lengthy periods of absence from Renate before the couple decided to give the separation permanency.

Elton has admitted that almost from their wedding day, professional schedules had dominated his life. If not recording, he was on tour. Free of concert engagements, Watford business became the paramount concern.

Yet once more (in the words of his album title) A *Single Man*, the indications were that, in improved health, the star needed no blandishments to resurrect his fiercely demanding working agenda.

Thus 1988 saw the release of *Reg Strikes Back*, the belated concert return in America, further recording in Denmark for the successor LP and no slackening in his obligations to Watford FC.

Utilising a football team's worth of familiar faces, *Reg Strikes Back* offered few surprises. No album of John-Taupin compositions neglects commercial sensibilities and 'I Don't Wanna Go On With You Like That' was one of a number of chart pretenders.

Again, the band essentially comprised the Live Aid line-up, augmented by guest appearances from Pete Townshend ('Town Of Plenty') and Beach Boys, Carl Wilson and Bruce Johnston ('Since God Invented Girls'). Harking back almost two full decades to the roots of Elton's fame, there were additional cameo slots for Dee Murray and Nigel Olsson.

Having passed its twentieth anniversary, Elton and Bernie's song-writing partnership is still capable of a prodigious and eclectic output.

Anyone charged with compiling a new 'best of' collection would have his work cut out sifting through half-forgotten classics accessible and emotive.

As far back as 1974, the redoubtable duo's repertoire was in excess of 150 songs.

Undeniably, Taupin's enforced spell in the wilderness in the late 1970s coincided with Elton's artistic and commercial nadir. It took the next complete album of John-Taupin compositions, *Too Low For Zero*, to restore the star to worldwide prominence.

In consequence, Elton has no cause to be anything but complimentary about his songwriting partner. Interviewed on breakfast television, he simply assessed the special chemistry between the two.

'I've never questioned the way it works. It's a great relationship. I can't ever think of me being without Bernie, not just in songwriting terms but as a friend. I think as much of him as I have always done.'

For his part, Bernie remains stoically content to write the lyrics, collect the royalties and shun the spotlight.

'I am in the shadow of Elton but I enjoy it,' he admits. 'I'm basically a very private person and would not want to be on the front page of newspapers every day.

'The blending between us now is so strong. I think we've never got on better.'

While Elton simultaneously consolidated his musical life and sorted out his personal one, it was his infamous possessions which garnered the headlines in the autumn of 1988.

Traditionalist auction house, Sotheby's went decidedly downmarket for its Elton John sale – basically the product of a mammoth house-clearing exercise at Elton's Windsor residence.

Items exquisite, exotic and extreme took Sotheby's removal men three days to clear from the house. A compulsive collector, his arts and crafts acquisitions reflected a well-travelled man with tastes untainted by convention.

Despite some works offensive to purists, the Sotheby's experts discovered many inspired purchases.

'I collected the art nouveau for £5,000-£6,000 back in the early seventies,' Elton recalled. 'I had no idea how much it would increase in value.'

The sale catalogue was itself something of a collector's item. Running to four lavish volumes embellished by portraits of the singer by top press photographer, Terry O'Neill, the £40 catalogue was the first marketed by Sotheby's through a retailer.

In a foreword, the Sotheby's chairman and former Arts Minister, Lord Gowrie, succinctly captured Elton's dilemma: 'He has simply out-collected his home's ability to absorb what he has purchased.

'When I first went there it was an Aladdin's cave, a magic toy shop.'

The first volume of the catalogue dealt with stage costume and incorporated 100 pairs of Elton's erstwhile trademark, the truly bizarre spectacles. Among the concert outfits was the spectacular Statue of Liberty number to commemorate the American bicentenary, while the catalogue also featured his jukeboxes and pinball machines.

The second volume was devoted to a highly individual range of 'famous names' jewellery; the third and fourth to the items of interest to the serious collector.

These included Rembrandt prints, a dazzling array of Carlo Bugatti furniture, and a collection of Viennese 1920s bronze and ivory sculptures of dancers, bathing belles, etcetera, acknowledged as one of the finest of its genre.

The seller doubtless approved of Sotheby's version of an advertising campaign. As though promoting an LP, the auction house took on tour highlights from the Elton John collection, visiting Tokyo, Sydney, New York and Los Angeles.

Moreover, the widespead interest in the sale preview at London's Victoria and Albert Museum led experts to debate whether Elton's income would benefit from what had been termed the 'Warhol factor' – translated as the increased value of objects connected with the famous.

Abetted by Sotheby's sagacious marketing, might the exceptional prices fetched by some of Andy Warhol's belongings auctioned in New York be repeated?

In the event, though the £5 million total exceeded by £2 million the estimated proceeds, Elton's sale fell shy of the Warhol league.

Nonetheless, a buyer was found for almost all the 2,000 lots – from fine art to 39 walking sticks.

The auction had its sublime moments, most memorably the sale of the largest platform boots ever worn by the star. Standing almost as high as the singer in his stockinged feet, the giant Doc Martens on which Elton perched precariously in the *Tommy* movie went for £11,000 – way surpassing the £1,200-£1,800 estimate.

The buyer was Stephen Griggs of the Northampton manufacturers of

Doc Martens, who happily confessed that he had been prepared to bid up to £15,000.

In the absence of the vendor, Mr Griggs was the star of the auction for the world's press, obligingly posing with the boots most definitely not designed for walking.

Other lots were mementoes of professional achievement or personal fulfilment.

For example, bidding went up to £41,800 (double the estimate) for a painting of people scurrying around the church at Moreton-in-the-Marsh, Gloucestershire. Elton had it purchased in 1972 as a reminder of a special train excursion for Rocket Records' staff.

Signed photos from the Apollo 15 astronauts to Britain's very own 'Rocket Man' fetched £2,100.

A Sotheby's spokesman said afterwards that while a sale with lots as low as £50 was a rarity for a prestigious auction house, 'it was fun for once being able to sell to the man in the street.'

Numerous friends and fans mingled with the serious bidders, causing the police to erect crash barriers around the Sotheby's premises.

Though the dedicated found bargains among the arts and crafts silverware, the unlimited purses of the Hard Rock Cafe in Los Angeles and the Superstars' Cafe Hall of Fame chain ensured that the items with the more personal 'Elton' cachet did not go for a song.

Gus Dudgeon had to fork out an incredible £2,950 for a blue denim cushion. A straw boater went for £825.

An octogenarian bidder failed to land a pair of silver leather platform boots for £3,600. The boots went Stateside for £4,950.

A pair of Elton's more flamboyant glasses fetched, £3,200, quad-rupling the estimate. But the star spectacles – neon-lit and spelling his name – were bought for a shade under £10,000.

A personalized signed photograph from Elvis Presley sold for £2,500. Even a Watford jersey autographed by team members made £800.

Describing his home, pre-auction, as a warehouse, Elton ration-alized the motivation behind the grand clearance as an opportunity for 'somewhere to sit as well as somewhere to stand. I want nice couches for my guests.'

The purge, however, stopped short of his favourite paintings, grand piano and beloved 'Goon Show' scripts.

And there were acquisitive signs that Elton was taking steps to replenish his cultural stocks. When Sotheby's celebrated glasnost by staging the first Western-style art auction in the Soviet Union, two purchases were made on the star's behalf.

Elton paid £44,000 for an impressionistic landscape by Svetlana Kopystyanskaya and the same amount for a painting of women by her husband, Igor. He had viewed the paintings when exhibited by Sotheby's in London.

Though his home-loving sentiments are genuine, Elton will have limited time to admire his new purchases in a less cluttered environment.

Following his American concert dates, 1989 afforded European fans the opportunity to witness the star's resplendent return to live performance.

Watford fans were forewarned not to expect the regular match-day presence of the chairman, especially as Elton's touring was partly to finance the buying of new players and ground improvements. 'I hope they appreciate that I'm doing my bit towards trying to put the club back in the first division.'

Nevertheless, the lure of a big game at Vicarage Road often proved irresistible.

When Watford played Nottingham Forest in the fifth round of the 1988/9 FA Cup, Elton took a sporting break from his Denmark recording sessions. A two-nil defeat by Forest was the chairman's miserly reward.

On the positive side, Elton exuded pleasure at a new sponsorship deal for the club, potentially worth £500,000, by delivery company, Eagle Express.

During the darkest days of his persecution by *The Sun*, the star had been perturbed at the possibility of the negative publicity in any way diminishing the homely image of the football club. Certainly, it appeared more than coincidental when rumours swiftly surfaced about Elton selling his interest in Watford.

In a contemporaneous interview, Elton confessed that the sympathetic public response had been reassuring: 'All the letters I got said "We don't care what you do in your private life" as long as at Watford I behave myself and represent the club properly, as I have always done.'

How gratifying latterly for Elton to hear an Eagle Express executive describe Watford – with its 'sound management and clean image' – as the only potential football sponsorship the company wanted to explore.

Down the years, Elton has expressed a variety of ambitions to occupy his restless mind after he reaches pensionable age as a rock 'n' roller. An expanded involvement in sports administration and buying a radio station are two which spring to mind.

A career in movies is another idea floated periodically with press kite-flying linking him to eccentric film roles.

Bernie Taupin perceives a new maturity in his songwriting partner, which has enabled Elton to come back from 'rock bottom.'

As a friend and admirer, Kiki Dee is convinced that further surprises are afoot.

'People like Elton are in a difficult situation. They are stars known for a definite talent, so it is hard for them to develop. I know Elton will want to remain active.

'He cannot really go into films. He is so much of a personality, the public wouldn't relate to him in another guise. But he is very bright and there are other areas – even business.

'At forty, you are only really halfway there. You can either get melancholy or open up your life and do amazing things. Knowing Elton, I am sure it will be the latter.'

Index

INDEX

INDEX

Epilogue

Another English summer. A group of American tourists forsake the accepted attractions for a voyage of discovery.

Their pilgrimage takes them up the Metropolitan Line, alighting at Northwood Hills. Out of the station, across the road and into the pub bearing the same name.

A friendly word with the bar staff and they are escorted to the back room where peacefully rests the piano on which Reggie Dwight bashed out Jim Reeves songs for customers. Six years later, that same rotund pianist was being hailed as the new messiah of rock.

Flashlights pop until all photo opportunites have been seized. The mission has been an unqualified success.

The Americans depart, the legend lives. And all because Fat Reg could do a mean Jerry Lee Lewis.

The Albums of Elton John

For DJM:

Empty Sky (1969)
Elton John (1970)
Tumbleweed Connection (1970)
17.11.70 (1971)
Madman Across The Water (1971)
Honky Chateau (1972)
Don't Shoot Me I'm Only The Piano
    Player (1973)
Goodbye Yellow Brick Road (1973)
Caribou (1974)
Greatest Hits Vol.1 (1974)
Captain Fantastic And The Brown
    Dirt Cowboy (1975)
Rock Of The Westies (1975)
Here And There (1976)
Greatest Hits Vol. 2 (1977)

Lady Samantha (1980)

For Rocket:

Blue Moves (1976)
A Single Man (1978)
Victim Of Love (1979)
21 At 33 (1980)
The Fox (1981)
Jump Up (1982)
Too Low For Zero (1983)
Breaking Hearts (1984)
Ice On Fire (1985)
Leather Jackets (1986)
Live In Australia (1987)
Reg Strikes Back (1988)
Film Soundtrack:

Friends (1971)